SAD LOVE STORIES

SAD LOVE STORIES

A Study in Manic-Depressive Illness

John T. Young

Geoffrey Corshum Press
Ada, Michigan

Printed in the United States of America

05 04 03 02 01 00   5 4 3 2 1

Library of Congress Catalog Card Number
99-93429
ISBN 0-9674201-2-1

To the memory of my father and mother

Contents

Figures

Foreword

John Young recalls leaving the hospital with his dad at fifteen following his first attack of bipolar illness. At that time he had been sick for seven months, and like any young person he was anxious to have doctors and hospitals behind him. It was natural he should ask whether there were any follow-up appointments with his psychiatrist, prescriptions he was expected to take, or counseling of any kind. "No," the doctor proclaimed, "No further appointments or medications were necessary because with this kind of illness when you are sick you are sick and when you are well you are well."

That advice was given several years ago. Today's psychiatrist would modify that earlier counsel by prescribing a mood maintenance drug, such as lithium, or one of the anti-convulsant drugs, Depakote or Tegretol; or the doctor might continue to prescribe an antidepressant for a significant period after the depression has lifted to improve the odds against recurrence. The use of these drugs between attacks of affective disease has been beneficial, but still does not provide the optimum level of care. The prognosis for the bipolar individual would be much brighter if he or she were educated in the disease, in its possible causes (including its biochemistry) and in preventative strategies. Modern medicine continues to be sorely lacking in this approach.

In this book John Young outlines an exhaustive list of potentially precipitating factors for bipolar disease extending from an excess of stressful recent life events to any number of psychological and physical disorders. The writer argues we need an approach to health and disease that encourages an awareness of causative factors. A strategy based on the irrefutable physiological fact that central to any one attack of illness is not the bacteria or virus or even genetic tendency, but the weakened resistance brought about by man's health-destroying living habits and emotional and physical stress. We need to acknowledge there are conditions that set us up for illness and do what we can to allay those conditions.

Young's study focuses on these underlying factors, on the conditions at play in the intervals between attacks. His emphasis is prevention. He explains, for example, that while serious depression and mania are genetic and biochemical this does not preclude the need for psychologists and talk therapy. Young does recognize the vital role of pharmacology, but he insists treatment must be pluralistic. Any therapy that will reduce stress is valuable: talk, nutrition, exercise, meditation, even therapeutic baths. To beat this disease you do many things, you do them consistently, and you take personal responsibility.

Sad Love Stories displays a special depth which flows naturally from the writer's background. John Young had that first serious attack of bipolar disease at fifteen, his second at eighteen, and has lived with this illness for forty years. In addition to his own long history with the ailment, Young has witnessed the illness in three immediate family members: his mother and two older siblings suffered the havoc of manic depression as well.

While others have written moving personal memoirs based on their experience with the disease, Young's book combines extensive personal and family experience with careful scholarship. A career educator and avid reader, Young takes pleasure in research. He has investigated the seminal scientific and professional studies and provides a readable account of what this disease actually is and the best treatments for it. In one of the book's most telling chapters, he shows the scientific relationship between stress and mental disturbance. An individual's response to a stressor involves the same pathways in the human endocrine system, the identical network of hormones and neurotransmitters, that determine emotional and mental stability. The connection between stress and emotional response is undeniable — as are the implications for the prevention and treatment of affective disease.

CURT J. CUNNINGHAM, D.O.,
Psychiatrist

Preface

Though I have read widely on mental health issues for several years, I began pulling together the material specific to this study in the spring of 1995. I am motivated by a desire to know all I can about this lifetime nemesis: I had my first severe depression as a high school freshman in 1957 (hospitalization and insulin coma therapy) and my second as a college freshman in 1961 (hospitalization and electroconvulsive therapy). To this point in my adult life I have remained relatively stable with only a periodic mild depressive state and only very occasional minor mania attacks.

While others have written effective personal memoirs of what one endures with this illness, the compelling interest for me is the disease itself, its comprehension and management. My desire to understand the illness extends to its biochemistry: if Prozac, Zoloft, lithium, and the so-called "anti-convulsants," and various other drugs effectively alter mood states, I want to know why. And what goes amiss in the body chemistry to necessitate these medicines in the first place? I also want to assess the potential of talk therapy, the current status of electroconvulsive therapy, the role of stress, and the possible benefits of meditation, exercise, and other forms of complementary medicine like nutritional supplements and the natural herbs. To answer these and other questions I set myself the task of investigating the best professional studies with the purpose of weighing this formal research against personal insights formed from observing the tendencies of bipolar disease in a parent, two siblings, and myself over a period of forty years.

The reader will soon discover recurring themes. For instance, I have a strong conviction that the individual who assumes some personal responsibility for coping with this illness will do much better. The manic-depressive individual must be ever vigilant: like the diabetic or recovering alcoholic he or she must manage the illness every single day. These individuals must accept that they are ill even when they are well; the disease in its very nature is cyclical and the next attack could be just weeks away. If attention is given on every well day as well as every sick day, the outlook for this disease can be very bright. The management of bipolar disorder has everything to do with personal integrity, with personal habits and self-discipline: it is only good sense that knowledge of self coupled with a concerted effort to learn all one can about the illness will produce results.

The manic-depressive must also be willing to adopt a variety of preventative strategies to stave off potential attacks. Much has been made of a genetic cause: this finding is important and useful, but the most respected studies imply the cause is multi-dimensional and the approach to prevention and treatment must also be broad-based and pluralistic.

Warning — Disclaimer

This study provides information on manic-depressive illness — also known as bipolar disorder. The author intends the guide not as a substitute for the professional services of medical practitioners but only as supplementary information.

It is not the purpose of the study to cover all the relevant and useful information available on the subject, but to complement and amplify other texts. I would urge the reader to examine as many of the books and articles extant on the disease as possible and to tailor the information to individual needs. Perhaps one function of this study, particularly the sections labeled "References" and "Further Reading" is to provide a current list of the vast array of first-rate scholarship available.

Bipolar disorder is not a one-dimensional illness. Anyone who wishes to gain even a preliminary understanding of it must be prepared to invest a significant amount of time and effort. While many scholarly articles and books on the subject are extremely worthwhile, no one of them — including this one — provides all the answers.

This study makes several suggestions for managing the disease — one of these encourages the use of nutritional supplements. This recommendation, like all the others, should only be implemented with the knowledge and help of a licensed physician.

Glossary

affective illness — mental disease that involves the emotions and mood.

co-transmitters — originally it was thought that one neurotransmitter system, say serotonin, prevailed with each neuron. Currently we believe that while one system might dominate, several systems can be functional in the same neuron simultaneously; and, it is common for neurotransmitter systems to pair off: the amine Dopamine (DA) with the peptide Enkephalin or the amine Norepinephrine (NE) with the peptide Somatostatin.

CRH (corticotropin releasing hormone) — a chemical controlled by the neurotransmitter, serotonin. When the bipolar patient is under stress and serotonin in short supply, the CRH will be the trigger for ushering inordinate amounts of cortisol into the blood.

cyclothymic — a form of bipolar disorder in which the mood swings are not severe.

endogenous — a mental illness, like bipolar disease, which involves the blood chemistry and tends to be inherited.

5-HT (5 hydroxytryptamine) — the chemical name for the neurotransmitter system, serotonin, which is involved in the regulation of many of the physiological processes which form the core symptoms of depression and mania.

G.A.S. (General Adaptation Syndrome) — Dr. Hans Selye's theory that our endocrine systems respond to stress in a three-stage process: (1) alarm; (2) resistance; and (3) exhaustion.

HPA (the hypothalamus, pituitary, and adrenal axis) — Located in the brain and, in the case of the adrenals above the kidneys, these endocrine glands are linked by a network of hormones and neurotransmitters vital to our understanding of bipolar disease.

homeostasis — the theory that health is dependent on a stable environment both within the body and without.

hypomania — a milder, more subtle form of manic behavior which we associate with cyclothymic or Bipolar II, but not Bipolar I, patients.

orthomolecular medicine — the theory that large doses of vitamins and minerals can neutralize genetic deficiencies and restore the body, physiologically and psychologically, to a normal or correct ("ortho") state.

peptide (neuropeptide) — strings of amino acids which have neurotransmitter actions; many of the most recently discovered neurotransmitters are peptides.

permissive hypothesis — the belief that the mania and depressive phases of bipolar illness are characterized by an undersupply of the neurotransmitter, serotonin.

pure consciousness — that state the mind reaches when it is allowed to gradually decelerate and rest until it attains that degree of profound quiet where it actually transcends thought.

schizophrenia — a form of mental illness distinct from manic depression in which the psychotic states are more severe and the periods of normality typical of bipolar disorder are missing.

serotonin — the neurotransmitter system in short supply in people with manic-depressive illness.

tryptophan — an "essential" amino acid that functions as a precursor to serotonin.

unipolar — those individuals who experience affective illness characterized by despair and depression but not mania.

Acknowledgments

I wish to give special thanks to Suzanne Elliott Vahey, a cousin by marriage and recently deceased. Sue and her father were both diagnosed manic-depressive. She was the first to encourage me to speak openly and frankly about my disease.

I wish to recognize as well the two psychiatrists who helped me get well following my two severe attacks with bipolar disease in 1957 and 1961:

> — Ken Nickel, M.D., of Butterworth Hospital (now Spectrum Main), Grand Rapids, Michigan.
>
> — Gordon Dietrich, M.D., of Mercywood Sanitarium, Ann Arbor, Michigan.

I would be remiss in mentioning Dr. Dietrich and Mercywood without, at the same time, saluting my two brothers. When paranoia prevented my accepting help from any source, my brothers personally "escorted" me the one hundred miles to the sanitarium.

I have also received help with the content and actual writing of the manuscript:

> — Thomas Blakely, Ph.D., a career professor of psychology with many years experience treating the mentally ill, made several

suggestions for improving the discussion of talk therapy in Chapter 9.

—Dr. Curt Cunningham (psychiatrist) and Dr. Gregory Dziadosz (psychologist) analyzed the manuscript with an eye to their respective specialties. Their positive response inspired the continuation of my study.

—Connie Smith, sister to a manic-depressive and mental health activist, examined an early draft and gently steered needed revisions.

—Dirk Nebbeling, a long-time instructor of writing in the schools and colleges, proof-read the book.

—Robert E. Young, for many years an administrator for the manufacture and sale of nutritional supplements, contributed to the chapters on nutrition and improved other content as well.

—Robert F. Yudin, D.D.S., dentist for the Transcendental Meditation community in Fairfield, Iowa, and his wife, Nora, have practiced meditation faithfully for over twenty-five years with excellent results both physically and emotionally. Their dedication and scholarship provided the inspiration for my discussion of meditation in Chapter 7.

I wish to recognize as well the hundreds of dedicated doctors and research workers who have contributed so much to our understanding of brain chemistry and manic-depressive illness.

I am just very grateful for the support of my wife, Judy, and maturity of my daughter, Christine, as I pursued this study.

JOHN T. YOUNG

On a huge hill
Cragged and steep, Truth stands, and he that will
Reach her, about must, and about must goe;
And what the hills suddenes resists, winne so;
Yet strive so, that before age, deaths twilight,
Thy Soule rest, for none can worke in that night.
To will, implyes delay, therefore now doe:
Hard deeds, the bodies paines; hard knowledge too
The mindes indeavors reach, and mysteries
Are like the Sunne, dazling, yet plaine to all eyes.

— John Donne, "Satyre III"

1 A Precipitating Factor

"The poignancy of situations which evoke reflection lies in the fact that we do not know the meaning of the tendencies that are pressing for action."

John Dewey, *Human Nature and Conduct*

During my second severe attack with manic-depressive illness at age eighteen, I was taken to a private psychiatric hospital, Mercywood Sanitarium, outside Ann Arbor, Michigan. For many years Mercywood has been considered a very fine institution boasting the best doctors and facilities. However, when I was taken to the hospital, I was detained in an underground, basement segment reserved for the most disturbed and depressed patients. I was restrained in this "lock-up" for several weeks while I endured a series of ten or twelve electroconvulsive (shock) treatments.

I recall those weeks in the basement of Mercywood as the most forbidding emotional moments of my life. Not only was I experiencing the chemical depression characteristic of the disease but also the terror and loneliness of being literally locked away in such a place while still

1

a teenager. But out of the despair of those moments evolved a state of mind and determination that have shaped my life ever since. That was over three decades ago, yet I vividly recall making the vow I would never allow the disease to bring me to that point again.

Making that vow in the basement asylum at Mercywood represented for me a moment of truth. I recalled leaving a similar facility four years earlier and asking my dad if the doctor recommended anything I could do to prevent a relapse with the illness. The doctor had told dad, "No, with this disease when you are well you are well and when you are sick you are sick." I just could not accept the degree of fatalism implied in the doctor's assessment for dad and decided if I was able to get back on my feet and leave the hospital, I would follow a course of action in direct opposition to what the doctor had implied to dad four years earlier. I would learn all I could about this illness and how to eliminate — or at least — significantly diminish its potential attacks. I was very fearful if I fell ill a third time with anything close to the severity of my first two attacks, I would not survive.

My history with manic-depressive illness began on a Tuesday night in February of 1957. I was still quite young — three months shy of fifteen. Like many boys in their early teens I loved athletics and played on the football, basketball, and tennis teams. Near the end of basketball season of my freshman year in high school, the coach put me in a game. When a teammate passed me the ball, I began a dribbling act and refused to pass the ball back to him or to any other of my teammates. This unusual behavior went on for several seconds before the coach surmised something was very wrong and removed me from the game.

Following the game, the rest of my teammates quickly showered, dressed, and headed for the bus. It was a weeknight game and we had school the next day. My abnormal behavior continued, however, as I removed my basketball uniform and just sat unclothed on a locker-room bench, refusing to shower. Fortunately, my dad was attending the game and came down to the locker-room. He and the coach finally convinced me to shower and dress. Later that night I was taken to the office of the team doctor, an internist, who prescribed tranquilizers.

What I had experienced in that basketball game as a high school freshman was clearly an episode of manic behavior. At the time it occurred, my mother was in a sanitarium fighting her way through a painful and enduring depression. While other family members and doctors surmised some connection between my mother's illness and my own, their inferences were vague and ineffectual. General terms like "nervous breakdown" or "neuresthenia" were still bandied about in 1957, and doctors were not yet emphasizing a genetic cause.

Normally a good student, I could not concentrate and focus on my studies through March and April and on through the rest of the term. I attended my final exams in early June but took all E's. Throughout that period in the spring of 1957 and into summer, I experienced many of the typical symptoms of the depressive mode: inability to sleep (particularly the early morning waking), worry, paranoia and irritability, weariness, physical depletion, and I was totally unrefreshed after sleep.

The doctors and my family didn't know what to do for me. They gave me tranquilizers to keep me under some control and hoped rest would gradually bring relief. During these early teen years, I typically spent my summers playing competitive tennis. I was not allowed to play tennis the summer of 1957 because it was believed tournament tennis would prove too stressful. By the beginning of August, there was no improvement and I had shown so much unhappiness and irritability the doctors decided on hospitalization.

So mother and I changed places. Just about the time her depression finally lifted and she was able to return home I entered "A-West," a ward of a local hospital specially created to treat mental illness. From the time I experienced the mania attack on the basketball floor in February until a two-week course in insulin coma therapy provided relief, I suffered through seven months of this illness. Because of advancements in diagnosing and treating bipolar disease, attacks of the illness such as I endured in 1957 should be less severe today. When articles and books suggest this illness is likely genetic, my family nods in strong agreement. Here we describe an attack of my own and one of my mother's, but my mother endured several other attacks of mania and depression both before and after the one alluded to above in 1957. I had my worst attack not in 1957 but in 1961, and an older brother experienced volatile mood swings in the mid-1970's and mid-80's as well. Though my sister was never formally diagnosed manic-depressive, her medical history strongly suggests she was. She experienced bouts with depression and emotional instability throughout her adult life and turned to alcohol as a form of self-medication. In the end, the alcohol became addictive, then toxic, and eventually led to cirrhosis of the liver.

The link from depression to alcohol abuse experienced by my sister is carefully documented in the literature. Ronald Fieve, M.D. and other prominent researchers specializing in bipolar disorder believe alcoholism is often a means of coping with the mood swings typical of this illness.

So, my mother, a brother, and very likely my sister suffered from the disease as well as myself.

A Record of Manic Depression in My Family

I. My mother (died, December of 1987)
   — (age 38) Spent several months in Wisconsin sanitarium for depression. Not sure of treatment.
   — (age 53) Spent nine months in Pine Rest Sanitarium in Grand Rapids, Michigan for depression. Treatment: ECT (Electroconvulsive Therapy).
   — (age 76) Spent one month in Forest View Psychiatric Clinic in Grand Rapids for mania. Treatment: lithium
   — (age 82) Again spent one month in Forest View Psychiatric Clinic for mania. Treatment: lithium

II. Older sister (died, November 1994)
   — Never formally diagnosed with manic depression, but died at 58 from alcoholism — a clear attempt to self-medicate for depression.

III. Older brother
   — (age, 39) Received help from Nathan Kline Clinic in New York for severe mood swings, both mania and depression. Treatment: lithium.
   — (age, 49) Prolonged depression. Treatment: In addition to lithium, various antidepressants (for example, monoamine oxidase inhibitors, Nardal, tricyclics). Antidepressants did not

prove effective after repeated trials and finally received series of ECT treatments. Recovery also seemed dependent on Aaron Beck's Cognitive Therapy.

IV. Myself
   — (age 15) Spent three weeks for mixed states in psychiatric ward in large metropolitan hospital in Grand Rapids, Michigan. Treatment: Insulin Coma Therapy.
   — (age 18) Spent three months at Mercywood Sanitarium in Ann Arbor, Michigan for mixed states (followed by depression). Treatment: ECT

Genetic Research Is Compelling

Genetic causes have been studied in moderate to severe cases of patients with manic depression. Twin studies suggest strongly that high rates within families are largely due to genetic factors. Thus, from a review of seven twin studies, Price (1968) concluded that the concordance rates for manic-depressive psychosis were 68 per cent for identical twins (97 pairs studied) reared together, 67 per cent for identical twins reared apart (12 pairs), and 23 per cent for non-identical twins (119 pairs). Similar percentages were reported in studies from Denmark (Bertelsen et al 1977).

Studies of adoptees also point to a genetic causation. In a study of 29 adoptees who had suffered from a bipolar affective disorder, Mendlewicz and Rainer (1977) found psychiatric disorder in 31 per cent of their biological parents (mainly but not exclusively affective illnesses), as against only 12 per cent of their adoptive parents.

With regard to this question of a genetic cause for manic depression, Ronald Fieve, M.D. wrote a telling letter to his former teacher and mentor at Columbia's Medical School, Professor Lawrence Kubie. Kubie had been of the Freudian school and believed bipolar disease the result of unresolved neurosis deeply embedded in the patient's past and the only plausible therapy extensive psychoanalysis (talk therapy). Fieve's experience as a young psychiatrist was leading him away from the thinking of his mentor and he explained his position in the following letter to Kubie.

"From the work we have done here it is my belief . . . manic-depressives have a strong genetic loading (i.e., predisposition). My impression is that lithium treatment dramatically eradicates or at least markedly attenuates over 80 per cent of future highs and lows in manic-depressives. Some of these, of course, are still left with personality disorders requiring psychotherapeutic or at times analytic treatment."

The thinking in Fieve's letter to Kubie was revolutionary as it implies heredity and brain chemistry (biochemistry) better explain major mood disorders than the traditional psychoanalytic explanation. This mode of thinking not only represented a difficult adjustment for Professor Kubie but for the entire field of psychiatry. In another place Fieve writes "...mania and mental depression must be due to biochemical causes handed down through the genes since they are correctable so rapidly by chemical rather than talking therapy."

2 A Brief History

"The management of troubled mood requires dedication, education, and personal insight. Beyond the contributions of the pill bottle and the sophistication of the brain sciences, self-knowledge is the key to regaining one's health."

— Peter Whybrow, M.D., *A Mood Apart*, 1997

Though the tendency late in the 20th century to process vital nutrients from our foods and to live with unprecedented stress will likely continue to increase the numbers with this disease, bipolar disorder is not new to man. The combination of environmental factors and body chemistry that account for the illness have likely existed, to one degree or another, from man's earliest history. While bipolar disorder and manic depression are current descriptive terms, not so long ago melancholia, neurasthenia, and nervous breakdown were more in vogue.

The terms melancholia and mania both originate with the Greeks and their use by Robert Burton in *The Anatomy of Melancholy* (1621) anticipate much of our understanding of the disease late in the 20th century. Burton described what he called the four humors in man. These humors referred to the tendency to feature one of four different personality types or moods and the mood that prevailed in any one individual was clearly, according to Burton, dependent on the preponderance of one humor or chemical (say bile) over the others. The best and most sophisticated modern research is simply a refinement of these early theories popularized in these much earlier writings by Robert Burton and others. We no longer talk about the black fluid,bile, spewed out by the kidneys or liver, but we do emphasize the role of hormones produced by the hypothalamus and adrenal glands.

And, while neurasthenia and nervous breakdown have also been dropped from modern parlance, they too are not wholly inappropriate descriptive terms. Neurasthenia literally means a weakness or depletion in the nervous system and recent research tells us bipolar disorder involves the neuroendocrine system and is very likely the result of an insufficient amount of the neurotransmitter, serotonin.

Though gradual progress was made in the description and diagnosis of this illness between the 17th and 20th centuries, it was not until 1921 that psychiatrist Emil Kraepelin introduced the term manic-depressive illness. Kraepelin concluded that the disease: 1) primarily involves the emotions; 2) occurs as a result of body chemistry; 3) can exist independently of other forms of mental illness — such as neurosis; 4) has a periodic or cyclic nature; 5) seems to have a genetic component; and 6) appears in individuals who seem to have a personality predisposition for it. Certain of these six Kraepelin conclusions have proven more accurate than others over the past seventy-five years, but they have all more or less held up. They are listed in the eighth edition of Kraepelin's textbook — still considered an authoritative text in psychology.

Nutritional and Biochemical Factors

While personality predisposition and genetic make-up can be underlying factors for bipolar disorder, the disease would never surface in any one individual if it were not for the second in Emil Kraeplin's six-part definition — that the disease occurs as a result of change in the body chemistry. Fortunately, through nutrition, stress reduction strategies, and drugs, we can regulate the relevant brain and endocrinal chemistry in those individuals susceptible to manic-depressive illness.

Nutrients can be extremely helpful with this disease and must assume a position of primary importance in its prevention and treatment. There is evidence that low levels of certain neurotransmitters, chemicals in the brain, are linked with depression. One of the amino acids, tryptophan, acts as a precursor to serotonin and requires the enzymatic action of vitamins B-3 and B-6 to maximize the production of serotonin in the brain. Though B-3 and B-6 function importantly with tryptophan, the B-complex vitamins work as a team and should be taken together. Folic acid, B-1, B-5, and B-12 are other B-complex vitamins thought to be especially helpful for those with bipolar disorder.

Other vitamins and minerals may be helpful as well. The mineral magnesium fights depression. Studies show vitamin C is beneficial in the prevention and management of manic-depressive attacks. Seafood, high in the trace mineral selenium, is known to elevate moods depending on a deficiency level in the individual. Selenium can be toxic, so intake must be carefully measured. While high levels of vanadium are linked negatively with bipolar disease, high levels of vitamin C will reduce those levels.

Stress and Psychological Factors

Inadequate knowledge of nutrition's potential to prevent incidence of this disease is typically compounded by problems with stress and various psychological disabilities. Stress appears to be a major factor in starting the process for many people and can build up within a month of the onset of the illness. Psychological treatment involves several kinds of psychotherapy. Cognitive therapy, currently enjoying a strong following, studies how the thought process or way of thinking perpetuates the depression and how to change those patterns. Interpersonal therapy uses relationships to help discover why and where the depression came from.

This emphasis on stress and psychological causation calls to mind the limitations inherent in any definition — even Kraepelin's 6-point description of manic-depressive illness. In points 2 and 3, Kraepelin claims the illness results from body chemistry and can exist independently of other forms of mental illness. While his emphasis is justified and useful, it needs to be modified. While Kraepelin was correct in calling bipolar disorder endogenic; that it is: hereditary, recurrent, comes from within, and effects the body chemistry, it is not correct to assume that the disease is not also reactive. Research clearly shows, for example, that an attack of mania or depression is typically precipitated by a stressful recent life event.

Perhaps a more useful division than endogenic versus reactive would be endogenic versus neurotic. Depression produced by neurosis would result mostly from one's thought processes — negative thinking — while endogenous depression would emanate more from body chemistry. The neurotic depressive would tend to respond more favorably to psychotherapy and the manic depressive or endogenous depressive to the various nutritional and drug therapies. But again while such distinctions are useful, they are also limited as any one patient could be essentially manic-depressive and yet neurotic too and a candidate for psychotherapy as well as drug therapy.

While our concern in this study is principally with manic depression and, therefore, with emotional illness largely the result of body chemistry and only secondarily with neurosis, this entire issue is complicated by the fact that neurosis itself can effect body chemistry. This is true because our neurosis is largely a response to various forms of stress, and a very high percentage of individuals with bipolar illness experience significant psychosocial stressors as part of their psychic past and/or just prior to their first eposides as well as later episodes of mania and depression (Basco and Rush 1996). Such stressors include bereavement, divorce, and job loss, but include many other forms as well.

Thus, when we use the phrase, "sick with worry," we mean just that. We literally effect our body chemistry and make ourselves sick not only by the thoughts that reflect life's stresses but by the body chemicals those thoughts effect. In one way of thinking, then, it is entirely arbitrary to separate manic-depressives and neurotics: almost all manic-depressives are neurotic to one degree or another. And, in the same way, it is arbitrary to divide endogenic and neurotic since they both effect body chemistry: the first through heredity and genetic markers and the second through stress and negative thinking. That portion of a manic-depressive's illness rooted in his or her heredity or genetic makeup (its endogenic aspect) might be the more telling cause, but neurosis so toxic as to poison body chemistry can be a powerful secondary component.

3 Making the Diagnosis

"The competent physician, before he attempts to give medicine to the patient, makes himself acquainted not only with the disease, but with the sick man."

— Cicero

An accurate diagnosis has to be the first step in attaining a positive outlook for one with bipolar disease. The advancement in effective medicines has been miraculous in the past quarter century, but these drugs are designed for specific forms of emotional illness. Precision in diagnosis, therefore, is a very high priority. A description of the mood shifts so basic to the illness is a good place to begin.

The typical manic-depressive will go from a period of unbridled enthusiasm, elation, or excitement to abject misery and the depths of despair. When in the depressed mode, he will demonstrate low self-esteem and have feelings of hopelessness. He will lack the incentive to make the smallest effort, even to get out of bed or go to work. Some individuals when depressed suffer from early morning waking; others want to sleep for weeks. They withdraw from social activities, avoid relationships with others, and frequently leave their jobs because of low energy and lack of self-confidence. The severely depressed can be suicidal.

When in the manic phase, these individuals will have what seems to be boundless energy. They will not want to rest or sleep for twenty-four hours or more. These periods of mania or excitement begin suddenly and without warning. Some realize these manic moods often; others can live years without a recurrence. Unlike most other illnesses that effect the mind, such as schizophrenia, manic-depressives return to normal behavior between stages.

Bipolar I and II

Mental health workers first began to use the term bipolar to distinguish those individuals suffering from emotional illness who demonstrated high or elated moods as well as the depression normally consistent with affective disease. Some studies reserved the term bipolar only for those patients who demonstrated manic symptoms so severe they required restraint and hospitalization; other studies broadened the term bipolar to characterize those with milder symptoms of mania as well. In 1976 Dunner and colleagues suggested bipolar patients could be better classified into bipolar-I and bipolar-II. Bipolar-I patients were defined as those with a history of mania severe enough to have resulted in treatment (usually hospitalization). This type of full-blown mania usually is consistent with psychotic features. Bipolar-II patients, by contrast, had in addition to major depression requiring hospitalization a history of hypomania (or mild mania) — which is to say, specific symptoms of sufficient magnitude to be designated as abnormal by the patient or the family and to result in interference in normal role functioning but not severe enough to be hospitalized solely on the basis of these mania symptoms.

In 1978 Angst refined Dunner's definition of bipolar by proposing a nomenclature that would account for milder forms of both depression and mania (see Figure 3-1). He divided bipolar patients into Md and mD, with M and D indicating an episode requiring hospitalization, and m and d designating episodes clearly different from normal but not of sufficient severity to necessitate hospitalization. Pa-

Clinical Construct

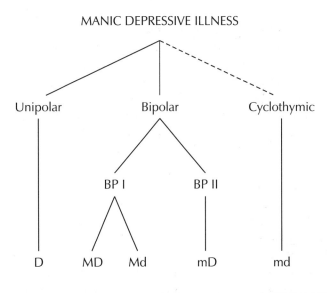

Figure 3-1. The Evolution of the Bipolar-Unipolar Distinction

tients who demonstrate these mild mood swings toward both poles are known as cyclothymic. Though their symptoms are mild, this group should be classified with manic-depressives because of their family history and response to medication.

Ever since bipolar illness was first witnessed, physicians and researchers have observed the many and varied forms it can take. This is especially seen in the length, frequency, and pattern of episodes. Some of these variations in pattern can be of great importance and represent distinct subtypes which determine the patient's experience with the disorder, and at times the doctor's approach to treatment.

These subtypes include **mixed states** (also called **mixed mania**) which is experienced by individuals who have episodes of both mania and depression daily for one week, are socially or occupationally impaired, and might require hospitalization. The patients may be sad and lacking energy but also irritable, or they might be manic and restless and yet feel an underlying melancholy. Mixed states may occur as independent episodes, but they are seen more often during transition from mania to depression or from depression to mania. During periods of transition the condition may alternate between mania and depression several times within the same day (Schou 1993). Other subtypes are **hypomania**, a less severe form of mania with limited functional impairment; **cyclothymia** (mentioned above), characterized by numerous, mild manic episodes and often less severe depressive episodes for at least two or more years with no major depressive or manic episode; and **rapid cycling.**

Rapid cycling is presently defined as four or more manic, hypomanic, or depressive episodes in any 12-month period. Depressive episodes are defined as lasting two weeks or longer; hypomanic episodes as lasting four days or longer; manic episodes as lasting one week or longer or requiring hospitalization. In some instances, episodes can be more frequent (and therefore of shorter duration). For some patients, rapid cycling is a temporary phenomenon. That is, they may exhibit rapid cycling for a time, then return to a pattern of longer, less frequent episodes. Other patients, however, may continue in a rapid-cycling pattern indefinitely.

While 60 to 80% of other individuals with bipolar disorder will experience significant relief from lithium, the response rate among those with rapid cycling is only 20 to 40%. It has been suggested that lithium's effectiveness might be reduced by drug or alcohol dependence, which is more common among those with the rapid cycling form of the illness, but this does not seem sufficient to account for the great difference in response rates. The disappointing results obtained with lithium in the treatment of rapid cycling led researchers to seek alternative treatments. When Depakote was approved in 1995 by the U.S. Food and Drug Administration (FDA) for the treatment of mania associated with bipolar disorder, it brought new hope to patients experiencing rapid cycling and mixed states. Tegretol (carbamazepine) also has been used successfully as a supplement or alternative to Depakote and lithium (National DMDA 1996).

Bipolar versus Unipolar

The unipolar patient, as the term implies, exhibits emotional instability toward only one pole — depression; and, the term was initially intended to signify just endogenous depression (that which involves the body chemistry). With many mental health practitioners, however, unipolar came to connote any depressed individual who had never experienced hypomania or mania — meaning unipolar applied not only to endogenous depression but to reactive and cognitive (neurotic) as well.

Major Depressive States

If we allow for individual differences in symptoms, in their number and kind as well as their degree, depression biologically based and consistent with bipolar disorder can be said to include the following:

- interruptions in sleep pattern (especially early morning waking);
  or
- a desire to sleep too much
- general restlessness; inability to concentrate and keep focused
- motor retardation, slow movement, lethargic
- loss of appetite and weight
- tired, weary, low energy
- damp and clammy hands and/or feet
- loss of confidence and self-esteem; easily overwhelmed
- loss of interest in most things (including sex)
- withdrawn, introverted, irritable, even paranoic
- suicidal

Mania Also Requires Diagnosis

While some individuals with mood disorder are truly unipolar as they only experience the depressive symptoms outlined above and never feature the mania side of the illness at all, the doctor needs to be aware of the entire spectrum of potential mood states in individuals subject to emotional disease. By persistent questioning of the patient, family, and even close friends, the practitioner can determine if there are bipolar tendencies.

The best research suggests, however, that doctors seldom take time to invite a patient to carefully examine and scrutinize his or her own psychic history to ascertain periods of elation and expansion as well as those of despair. This could account for the seemingly high number of unipolar depressives. It very well could be that more thorough diagnostic practices would result in many of the so-called unipolar depressives being re-classified as bipolar. This inability to properly classify many unipolars coupled with the sizeable number with affective disease who are never diagnosed at all likely accounts for most studies listing only 1 % or 2.7 million Americans with manic-depressive illness. Here are some of the most common symptoms of a manic-depressive in the high or "manic" mode:

- occasional delusions; some tendency to hallucinate
- grandiose ideas
- high energy and creativity ("reved" or "torqued" up/ racing thoughts)
- outlandish buying sprees
- heightened sociability and talkativeness (manics tend to call people all over the country suffering astronomical phone bills); talk is not only expansive, but rapid — and manics want the last word
- increased sexuality (typically, appropriately directed — but sometimes to the point of promiscuity as marriages and relationships can be tragically destroyed)
- eccentric, atypical behavior
- extreme irritability and hostility — even violence

As in the depressed phase, the symptoms of the manic pole vary widely from individual to individual; some manic-depressives engage in truly freakish — and very often costly — modes of behavior while in the manic mode (bipolar-I): for others, the swing in this direction is much more subtle and much more difficult to detect as an aberration from normal behavior (bipolar-II). In most cases, however, the persistent practitioner can help the patient discover "manic" episodes in his or her psychic past and, thereby, augment the diagnostic process.

Mania Can Be an Advantage

We must not conclude, however, that manic states are always negative. Kay Jamison, Ph.D., herself a psychologist and manic-depressive, has written a book, *Touched with Fire*, that centers entirely on manic depression and the artistic temperament. Jamison suffered horribly from the disease before she discovered what the illness is and how to cope with it. In spite of her many years of suffering and several suicide attempts, Jamison has learned to appreciate singular qualities in those with bipolar disease. She believes these individuals can have greater sensitivity and depth and range of feeling. She points out that some of our greatest writers, from Lord Byron to Ernest Hemingway, are clearly manic-depressive. And, she walks us through entire lists of musicians and painters whose biographies reveal bipolar disease as well.

In his study, *Mood Swing*, psychiatrist Ronald Fieve makes a strong case for a link between manic depression and creative work of all kinds. The playwrite, Josh Logan, wrote his most brilliant musical, *South Pacific*, while on a manic high. Abraham Lincoln, perhaps our greatest president, experienced patterns of behavior thought to be indicative of this illness. So mania can be an asset if kept in a moderate range (see the Fieve-Dunner Manic-Depressive Mood Scale at the end of this chapter), but it can be destructive and nightmarish if it soars to the highest ranges of hypermania or sinks to the lowest depths of its polar opposite, suicidal depression. Hemingway wrote some of the world's best short stories and novels while mildly manic, but more than once he tried to jump out of an airplane enroute to the Mayo Clinic for electroconvulsive therapy and ultimately ended his own life by blasting the back of his head off with a rifle.

Subtlety Impairs Diagnosis

Mania attacks, particularly the milder forms of mania, can be very situational and occur innocently, with short notice, and such episodes are not necessarily dangerous in themselves or imply severe illness at the time; and yet, they do suggest the kind of sensitive endocrine system common in those with bipolar disease. These milder episodes of mania can so proximate normalcy that only the individual perpetrating the

17

behavior (or someone extremely close) will suspect any aberration. Another one of my experiences as a high school basketball player illustrates this extreme subtlety of some mania attacks and how difficult they can be to detect. Our high school team was dead-locked in a 52-52 tie score with an arch rival in a neighboring town; it was the winter break with young people home for the holidays and the fieldhouse packed to capacity. Soon after the coach put me in the game, I launched an inordinately long shot that broke the tie score and changed the momentum of the game in our team's favor. (Please keep in mind, these were the days prior to the introduction of the "3 point rule" when every shot, regardless of its distance from the basket, was awarded just 2 points).

Many a high school, college, or professional athlete has experienced that spurt of adrenalin which allows them to temporarily perform at a higher level, make the big play, and inspire their team — but this situation was different. Typically, a basketball team adopts either a zone or a man-to-man defense. Against a zone, the offensive team will quite often take reasonably long shots because they must shoot over the zone, but with a man-to-man the strategy is to maneuver for much shorter shots with an appreciably higher percentage of accuracy. Our opponent was clearly in a man-to-man defense when the score was knotted at 52 and I fired my 30-foot bomb. Had I missed that shot, the coach would have immediately taken me out of the game, sat me on the bench, and given me a sound lecture on the fundamental strategies of playing the game.

It is a wonder I should ever have attempted a shot of that kind. By nature I tend to be quiet and conservative; moreover, the modest gifts I had for playing basketball centered on defense and teamwork and not individual shooting and scoring. But the excitement and tension of the moment apparently induced a temporary mood of manic euphoria and I had an unshakeable confidence I could break the tie. So the highly sensitive endocrine system, characteristic of those with bipolar disorder, can at times allow unique, creative, and exceptional responses to moments of challenge.

But this experience was irrational and eccentric as well as unique and creative. When moments like these represent enough of a departure from the individual's normal pattern of behavior, they need to be uncovered as part of the patient's psychic history. Yet doctors rarely take the time to explore manic experiences like mine. They interview their patients when they are depressed, often in an extreme state of depression, never uncover mania experiences from the patient or family and falsely diagnosis true bipolars as unipolar depressives. This inability to properly distinguish between an actual bipolar and the unipolar depressive can be costly as it will alter the method of treatment and impede the course of recovery. My history of mildly manic incidents such as this one coupled with bouts of depression ranging from mild to severe suggests a diagnosis of Bipolar-II. As a result, my doctors prescribe lithium which has an excellent track record as a maintenance drug for those with bipolar disease.

We want to identify bipolars whenever possible because we have developed medicines (such as lithium) specific to this form of the disease. We have also developed medicines very effective in the treatment of the unipolar depressive wing of manic-depressive illness, but these are typically not the same as those used to treat bipolar illness.

Case Histories

Three case histories take symptoms out of the abstract and place them in a personal context. Susan and Robert, like myself, are clearly bipolar; Ted's is a difficult diagnosis as he demonstrates signs of bipolar disorder while he is actually schizophrenic.

Susan

Susan, a 24 year-old graduate student and aspiring professor, had been admitted to a university hospital psychiatric ward suffering from delusions and hallucinations. Over the previous four to six months her roommate had begun to observe changes in her behavior. Although usually down-to-earth and very objective in assessing her own abilities, Susan began talking about her brilliant future as a researcher and scholar and that she would soon complete an important book. When a friend pointed out that Susan struggled with routine graduate work and had never achieved any particular academic distinction, she became defensive and said her friend was merely jealous of her talents.

A short time later Susan began keeping late hours, supposedly

19

writing her book. Her mother became increasingly suspicious when Susan started calling her asking for money to cover numerous phone bills and a variety of other debts. She was becoming increasingly irritable with friends and classmates. One day she had a very disagreeable verbal fight with her professor over the proper interpretation of a literary passage. Also, about this time she commenced drinking more and more, claiming she could not fall asleep until she had consumed several beers. A week before being brought to the emergency room, Susan attempted to walk into the office of the university dean demanding a special fellowship to complete her book, had sex with four different men, spent $3000 in one morning on clothes, and made eight long-distance phone calls to a former boyfriend now living in Prague. Ultimately, her roommate called her parents one night in terror: Susan had been up the entire night drinking and making phone calls. Now she was threatening to bomb the office of the dean for not providing the fellowship for her book. Susan felt she was in direct contact with God and God wanted her to be granted this fellowship. In short, Susan had lost touch with reality.

The emergency room psychiatrist was able to diagnose bipolar affective disorder, the mania phase, after asking Susan's parents a few targeted questions. At age 18, they told the doctor, Susan had developed a mild-to-serious depression and at age 22, just after graduation from college, she relapsed with a similar depression.

So Susan had experienced at least two episodes of depression and now an attack of mania. Between these periods, she had been a responsible, diligent — though never brilliant — student. She had maintained a steady relationship with a boyfriend and she had been a loyal and sensitive friend and roommate. Further probing into Susan's psychic past and her family history revealed an aunt had experienced similar highs and lows and had been treated successfully with lithium for years.

Susan's case is instructive in, at least, two ways. First, the drinking pattern is typical of the manic stage. The consumption of inordinate amounts of alcohol could be an attempt by the manic to calm down and to deal with energy and emotions he or she can neither control nor understand. The drinking merely compounds the problem as the already peculiar and eccentric behavior can be made worse by the alcohol; and, until the manic sobers up and the effect of the drinking wears off it is difficult to assess the true symptoms of the disease and treat them. Second, without the doctor's knowledge of Susan's previous episodes with depression and also her periods of normal behavior between the highs and lows, it would have been very difficult for him to distinguish between schizophrenia and the proper diagnosis of manic-depressive illness. When we consider the details of Susan's behavior when she presented to the emergency room, we can easily see why she could have been diagnosed schizophrenic. At that moment, she was hallucinating and delusional, paranoid and violent. She firmly believed she was in direct contact with God. Had it not been for the doctor reaching out to the family and their coming forth with the vital psychiatric history of both Susan and her aunt the diagnosis could easily have been missed and the proper treatment long delayed.

Robert

Robert's case is also a study in mood swing but somewhat different than Susan's. He had been experiencing difficulties carrying out his duties as a bank executive and presented with the classic symptoms of depression: early morning waking, increasingly withdrawn and introverted, loss of weight and energy, decreased sex drive, and an inability to concentrate. Now, at age 35, Robert was seeking the help of a psychiatrist for the first time. He had, however, seen a psychologist intermittently for several years, and the talk therapy had been moderately effective in stabilizing mood swings. Because the psychologist feared Robert's condition was deteriorating, he referred him to a psychiatrist who was professionally licensed to help Robert lift the depression with medication.

Soon after reporting to the psychiatrist, Robert's depression became acute and he was hospitalized. The psychiatrist tried many of the standard antidepressants on Robert: Prozac, Zoloft, the monoamine oxidase inhibitors, and the tricyclics — but these had little effect. Robert finally responded to a series of electroconvulsive treatments. As Robert's mood began to improve and he was able to converse in a more rational, normal way with his psychiatrist, it was possible to explore his psychic history in depth. During this process, the psychiatrist discovered Robert had not only suffered this recent complete collapse and earlier serious depressions but also had experienced periods of mania extending for two or three months over the past several years — not as severe as Susan's, but behavior clearly not normal. During these manic periods, Robert became extremely emotional, that is, he would laugh uproariously at only moderately humorous situations and burst into tears a short while later. He would talk excessively and become irksome at the slightest provocation with staff people at the bank. He slept badly, was nervous and distracted, and spent too much money. On several occasions during these highs, Robert was flirtatious with young women employees at the bank, tried to line up dates, and in one instance even had an affair. This behavior was not typical of Robert who felt strongly about the need to remain faithful to his wife and family, whom he loved very much. He felt extremely guilty about the affair, but when manic he claimed his sexual urges were beyond his control.

Unlike Susan, Robert never became psychotic while in the manic state. He did not hallucinate or become delusional or believe he had a special relationship with God. Still, he did say and do things he knew were foreign to his character — actions for which he was somewhat embarrassed and ashamed.

When the psychiatrist weighed the evidence of these mild mania attacks against the severe depression Robert had just endured, along with the history of serious depression, bipolar-II seemed the logical diagnosis. And, while electroconvulsive treatment had been necessary to lift his recent depression, the hypomania suggested lithium would be an effective maintenance drug.

Some could argue Robert's highs were so close to normal behavior, so harmless in their effect both on himself and others they simply did not require medication. After all, society expects executives to be irksome and demanding at times and while it is certainly neither proper nor right, it has become almost prosaic for bosses to have affairs with women at the office. But the psychiatrist knew Robert was sick during these cycles of mild mania just as he was when depressed. Mania can lead to much unhappiness and loss even though the patient might feel energized and exhilarated during these periods. On numerous occasions, manics have made disastrous financial deals believing themselves especially creative, inventive, and shrewd — only to discover how incredibly foolish they have been when the mood fades. Or like Robert, the manic becomes objectionable with other employees at the office or has an affair and risks getting fired from his job or ruining a marriage. Thankfully, Robert sought the help of a competent psychiatrist who understood lithium's potential to help him eliminate the extreme swings in mood that threatened to destroy his life.

Ted — A Difficult Case

Ted was a bright high school student and a fine athlete — a state champion in wrestling his senior year. Both of Ted's parents were professional people, one an architect and the other a physician. Throughout high school Ted excelled in all his subjects and seemed to reflect the intelligence of his two gifted parents. Outside of some occasional moodiness and a periodic tendency to seclude himself from his friends, Ted had an entirely normal high school experience.

Following high school, Ted went East to a fine ivy league school where he planned to continue his outstanding career in wrestling and pursue the study of medicine. He made an excellent adjustment initially, but during the second term his moodiness returned — only now the highs and lows were more intense. At times, he would be so depressed as to be suicidal. On other occasions he would become paranoid and delusional: he would hear distinct voices saying odd things; such as, "this food is poisonous." There were instances, too, when Ted would appear locked in a world entirely his own; he would giggle or laugh for no apparent reason.

Once this kind of behavior began to surface that second semester of his freshman year, Ted's health never returned to normal. In April, he was forced to leave college, he relocated in California, and drifted from job to job. Two years later when he should have been in his third year in college and well on his way to completing his undergraduate work in pre-med, an old high school friend found him living in a cheap hotel in a Los Angeles slum and eating out of garbage cans.

Ted's case is different from the others we've considered. He did experience moodiness in both high school and college, but the psychotic aspects of Ted's illness were considerably more severe than even the worst mania of a bipolar-I patient. While the manic hears voices that reflect his grandiose perceptions, he does not endure the crazed messages Ted experienced.

Ted was diagnosed a schizophrenic and was treated with lithium and a strong drug for the schizophrenia (thorazine). Unlike Susan and

Robert, Ted's mental condition gradually deteriorated: he did not enjoy those returns to mental equilibrium that characterize manic-depressives. Ted was never able to maintain a responsible job. His medication did, however, allow him to spend most of his life free of hospitalization.

Pursue Good Professional Help

Because much of the pain and suffering characteristic of bipolar illness can largely be eradicated today, it is important we learn to identify the signs and symptoms of the disease as represented in cases like those of Susan and Robert and to identify differences from other forms of mental disease as in the schizophrenia observed in Ted. The growing trend toward "managed care" and the tendency to spend even less time with patients makes it especially important those suffering from mood disorders — and the family members and friends providing their support — persevere with the diagnostic process. There is no substitute for consulting with a good psychiatrist and psychologist — and, in some instances, it might take more than one doctor from each of these specialties. The Fieve-Dunner Manic-Depressive Mood Scale presented at the end of this chapter rates the symptoms of the disease according to severity and indicates when hospitalization is required.

Far Too Many Go Undiagnosed

A recent study in the United States claimed a group of women posing as depressed patients fooled more than half the primary-care doctors they saw, pointing to a need for more time to be spent with patients. The $100,000 study, funded by the National Institute of Mental Health and conducted by the University of Alabama, took 16 women ages 35 to 55 and trained them to mimic four scenarios of depression, says Dr. Lee Badger, an associate professor in the UA School of Social Work.

To keep from tipping off doctors that the study was based on depression, one woman had a legitimate medical problem, Lupus.

"We trained them to enact the role of five patient cases," says Badger. "One had a medical condition. Four had major depression."

Forty-seven doctors from Alabama, Mississippi, and Georgia

agreed to the study, which included videotaping their interviews with the women. Each doctor was given the results of any medical test he wanted to order. Generally, the tests were negative.

The results of Badger's study found that between 50 percent and 80 percent of physicians did not recognize major depression.

Badger said that doctors who spent more time with patients — as much as 15 minutes — were more likely to recognize depression. But physicians on average spent only five to seven minutes with each patient.

"The amount of time a physician has with a patient is directly related to the probability to make a correct diagnosis," Badger added.

"Some terminated the interview after five or six minutes," she said. "If it went 15 minutes they generally made the (correct) diagnosis."

With the advent of HMO's and stricter requirements on doctors, many have less time to meet with patients. And rural doctors are pressed for time because of the numbers of patients they must see each day.

Badger's finding at the University of Alabama that 50 to 80 percent of physicians fail to diagnose major depression has very serious consequences. Untreated depression, for example, is thought to lead to 70 percent of the 30,000 suicides in this country every year. In addition, the flawed concentration typical of a depressed state accounts for many fatal accidents. Deaths from alcohol and other forms of abuse can be blamed on untreated depression. Society is also victimized as families are adversely affected and productivity in the work place is decreased through absenteeism, job-related injuries, and the lack of efficiency in the work environment.

Best Treatments Get Little Use

Although scientific knowledge about diagnosing and treating both mania and depression continues to grow, "there is a large gap between what treatment for emotional diseases can do and what is actually done in practice," said an advisory panel to the National Depressive and Manic-Depressive Association in a new report.

Late in the 20th century, the general public continues to misunderstand and stigmatize mental illness. One survey, for instance, reported that up to 65 percent of the general populace believe mental illness is caused by faulty parenting. Another 45 percent blame the disease on the sufferer, claiming it is a mere weakness that can be overcome with effort. Forty-three percent of those surveyed had a strong conviction that mental illness cannot be cured. Up to 35 percent deem mental illness the result of sinful conduct, and a paltry 10 percent believe the illness has a biological basis and involves the brain.

Some reasons that people with depressive illnesses aren't getting the care they need include: this continued social stigma attached to mental illness, lack of public awareness of symptoms and lack of cooperation among primary care physicians, psychiatrists, psychologists, nutritionists, and other mental health providers.

Two-thirds of people suffering from depression in the industrialized countries of the western world never get treated for the disorder. Half of this group never seeks any treatment, the rest seek medical help for their most common symptom: fatigue, anxiety, insomnia, stomach problems or loss of weight.

It is also believed patients and their family members underestimate the severity of depression and, therefore, do not pursue treatment (J. Endicott 1995). The same study concluded that individuals with major depression who did not seek treatment thought they could handle or treat the episode themselves. Furthermore, they did not see the episode as serious enough to seek treatment; they merely thought it was an expected response to a life situation.

Those individuals who do recognize the need for help might confront restricted access to treatment. This can be particularly true in parts of our country underserved by physicians and mental health care providers.

Moreover, patient compliance is a significant deterrence to adequate care; in other words, one's willingness to remain with a recommended medical regimen for the treatment of depression. This lack of adherence on the part of the patient can lead to inadeqate treatment and often to demoralization of the primary care physician.

On the other hand, many reasons for improper treatment reside less with the patient than with the physician. As we have observed above with the University of Alabama study, the responsibility for diagnosing and treating affective disease often falls on the primary care physician and not the more specialized psychiatrists. But many medical schools do not offer thorough study in psychiatric diagnoses, psychopharmacology, or psychotherapy for depression. Even post-graduate work for these primary care providers might be very superficial in these highly specialized psychiatric studies.

As a result of restricted training, the physician might be ill-prepared to tend their patients with the most modern methods. It might also be the case that the physician will lack the interpersonal skills necessary to manage emotional distress. This discomfort can lead many physicians to avoid tending those with affective disease.

In some instances, too, our primary care physicians might conclude that psychiatric disorders are not "real" illnesses. This untruth gains credence from the lack of good, objective markers for psychiatric disorders. Other providers might accept the reality of psychiatric disorders and even their capacity to inflict pain and suffering, but fear they would alienate their patients by bringing it up.

And, as we observed in the University of Alabama study, time is an important factor with psychiatric disorders. The Alabama study and several others imply primary care physicians either have too little time or do not take the needed time to effectively treat those with emotional diseases.

Easily Confused with Anxiety Attacks

While manic depression can be confused with schizophrenia, reactive depression, various phobias and illnesses, it is equally important we perceive its difference from anxiety attacks. Anxiety states occur as a separate syndrome from the depression of bipolar disease; for example, as obsessive states or panic disorders. The symptoms of anxiety states are mainly those of excessive stimulation of the sympathetic nervous system (autononomic hyperactivity). The inner tension characteristic of these anxiety states results in sleep disturbance which, in contrast to minor depression, is a problem of initial insomnia; in other words, the patient has difficulty falling asleep, but having eventually fallen asleep he or she has no difficulties in maintaining sleep. In minor depression symptomatic of bipolar disease, conversely, there is typically no initial insomnia but middle or late insomnia.

Fieve-Dunner Manic-Depressive Mood Scale*

(To be filled out independently by nurses and patients)

100 Medical emergency. Wildly manic and psychotic; can't stop talking; incoherent, overactive, belligerent, or elated. Not sleeping at all. At times delusional; hallucinating. May be either violent or paranoid.

90 Extreme elation so that patient can't rate self; in need of more medication and control. Completely uncooperative.

80 Severe elation. Should be admitted, or if in hospital usually wants to sign out of ward. Sleeping very little; hostile when crossed; loss of control. Needs medication.

70 Moderate elation. Overactivity and talkativeness; irritable and annoyed. Needs only four to six hours sleep. Socially inappropriate; wants to control. Outpatient treatment has been advised by doctors.

60 Mildly elevated mood and many ideas for new projects; occasionally mildly obtrusive. If creative, the energy is highly useful. Hyperperceptive. Feels wonderful, on top of the world. Increased sexual drive; wants to spend money and travel. Treatment may be contraindicated or not needed.

50 Mood is within normal range (45-55).

40 Mildly depressed mood, but noticeable lack of energy; chronic lack of optimism and pleasure. Feels slowed down. Treatment

---

The minor depressive states can be distinguished clinically from anxiety states if the physician recalls the esssential triad of bipolar depression: the mood of depression, decreased motor activity, and negative beliefs (lowered self-esteem). In minor states this triad manifests itself by symptoms such as lack of interest, fatigue, work impairment, introversion, and indecision. Recent studies have shown that both social impairment and decreased appetite are more typical of minor depressive states than anxiety states.

may not be desired, although it may be indicated. Decreased interest in sex. Decreased motivation.

30 Moderate depression. Loss of energy; disinterested in others; early weight, sleep,and appetite disturbance; able to function with effort but prefers, if possible, to stay in bed during day; doesn't want to go to work, but may force oneself; feels life is not worthwhile. Little sexual interest. Outpatient treatment advised by doctors.

20 Severe depression. Takes care of daily routine but needs prodding and reminding; loss or gain of weight; sleep disorder is serious. Volunteers suicidal feelings; very withdrawn, may be paranoid.

10 Extreme depression. Actively suicidal, totally withdrawn or extremely agitated. Difficulty rating self on mood scale.

0 Medical emergency. Unable to eat or take medication; can't follow ward routine; delusional, suicidal. Stuporous. Stares into space; very little response to questioning. May require tube feeding.

*Drs. Fieve and Dunner estimate that patients in the extreme ranges on the scale, 100 to 80 at the manic end and 0 to 20 on the depressed side, are typically candidates for hospitalization. Patients in the 20 to 80 range sometimes require hospitalization, but are often treatable on an outpatient basis. The patients in this moderate middle range are frequently capable of helping to rate themselves on this scale; those in the manic and depressive extreme ranges require the assistance of nurses and psychiatrists in this rating process.

4 Stress and the Neurotransmitters

"Stress is the state manifested by a specific syndrome which consists of all the nonspecifically inducted changes within a biologic system."

Hans Selye, *The Stress of Life*, 1956

Recently, molecular genetic methods have made possible the identification of specific genes for genetic disorders. While chromosomes 11 and X have shown promise in the search for genes specific to bipolar illness, subsequent studies have repeatedly resulted in disappointment. Yet faith remains strong that current methods will ultimately prove successful. A number of genes for diabetes have been mapped by a systematic genome survey of a large collection of affected sib-pairs. Accordingly, my brother and I are now participating in a similar sib-pair study for bipolars conducted by John Kelsoe, M.D., et al. of the University of California at San Diego. While we should anticipate results of studies like Kelsoe's with great hope and optimism, we should also be aware of those secondary causes for this disease that tend to exacerbate these very genetic markers we are seeking. Stress is one such secondary cause.

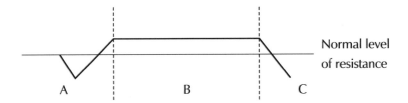

A. Alarm reaction. The body shows the changes characteristic of the first exposure to a stressor. At the same time, its resistance is diminished and, if the stressor is sufficiently strong (severe burns, extremes of temperature), death may result.

B. Stage of resistance. Resistance ensues if continued exposure to the stressor is compatible with adaptation. The bodily signs characteristic of the alarm reaction have virtually disappeared, and resistance rises above normal.

C. Stage of exhaustion. Following extended exposure to the same stressor, to which the body had become adjusted, eventually adaptation energy is exhausted. The signs of alarm reaction reappear, but now they are irreversible, and the individual experiences serious illness and possible death.

Figure 4-1. The Three Phases of the General Adaptation Syndrome (G.A.S.)

Hans Selye

As a young doctor Hans Selye, a professor of medicine at the University of Montreal, had been struck by the tendency of so many individuals to demonstrate identical physical symptoms though their specific maladies were very different. From this early observation, Selye began a series of many scientific experiments and studies eventually leading to an important new medical discovery: the general adaptation syndrome (G.A.S.). Its three stages: (1) the alarm reaction; (2) the stage of resistance; and (3) the stage of exhaustion — are illustrated in Figure 4-1.

Selye's theory quickly drew attention because it is such an inspired scientific explanation of what happens to the human body under stress. His discoveries explained the actual biochemical changes occurring in the body during traumatic periods. The implications of Selye's theories are not meant to suggest we live without stress — the only way to avoid it would be to do nothing at all. Virtually all human activity involves some conflict — from a game of bridge to a love affair. But this can be defined as the conflict of pleasure and fulfillment. What we all want is the right kind of challenge for the right length of time — at a level best for us. Excessive or unvaried stress, particularly frustration, becomes distress. And this, in turn, can lead to ulcers, hypertension, and mental disease.

Selye's ideas on stress and his general adaptation syndrome evolved from the thinking of the great French physiologist Claude Bernard. During the second half of the 19th century — before anyone had conceived a notion of the effect of stress on the body, Bernard maintained that the internal environment (the milieu interieur) of a living organism must remain constant, despite changes in its external environment.

Some fifty years later, the distinguished American physiologist Walter B. Cannon supported Bernard's argument when he wrote, "the coordinated physiological processes which maintain most of the steady states in the organism "should be called 'homeostasis' (from the Greek homoios, meaning similar, and stasis, meaning position), the ability to stay the same, or static. Homeostasis might be roughly translated as 'staying power.'"

Drawing on these insights of Bernard and Cannon, Selye wrote, "My milieu interieur is me — or at least the environment in which all my cells live. In order to maintain a healthy life, nothing within me must be allowed to deviate far from the norm. If anything does, I will become sick or even die" (Selye 1974).

Psychiatrist and researcher Peter C. Whybrow connects the importance of this concept of homeostasis to the emotional centers of the human brain. "Emotional behavior," writes Whybrow, "is a homeostatic system; it balances our interaction with the world, especially the social world in which most of us live. Such homeostatic systems are essential to life. Probing the natural order of living creatures, we find them everywhere, from the smallest cell to the most complex society. In fact, much of science, from molecular biology to sociology, is concerned with the study of such systems and their regulation.

"It is an essential characteristic of all homeostatic systems that they continuously strive to find the best fit with the environment within which they operate. An everyday example in the mechanical world is the thermostat, which governs the temperature of a room. As the room temperature changes, the thermostat makes the necessary correction by switching the furnace on and off, thus maintaining equilibrium around the temperature to which it has been set — technically known as the set point. The same general principles apply in biology, and in the human brain. Homeostatic systems are self-correcting in pursuit of optimum balance."

Whybrow explains that in mood disorders there is probably "no simple cause sufficient to explain the disease but rather there are many factors, including an inherited — that is, a genetic — vulnerability that can place somebody at risk. Changes in the body and the environment that profoundly impact brain regulation — generally we call these stressors — will dramatically drive behavior toward disorganization, while events that foster regulation and organization will return harmony and balance" (Whybrow 1997).

Recent Life Events

It has been believed for a long time that depressive disorders might be induced by stressful life events. However, researchers put up a number of red flags before we necesssarily conclude a direct cause and effect relation. First, the association might be merely coincidental: viz., *a* might occur simultaneously with *b*, but that does not establish a causal relation. Secondly, the association might be non-specific; there might be as many stressful events in the weeks preceding other kinds of illness. Thirdly, the association might be spurious; the patient might have regarded the events as stressful only after the fact when seeking an explanation for his illness, or he might have experienced them as stressful only because he was already depressed at the time (Gath 1983).

Through the use of sophisticated research methods, Paykel et al, in 1974, and Brown and Harris, in 1978, were able to show that recent life events can, in fact, contribute to the onset of depressive disorder. Though his findings are incomplete, Brown advanced what he called the "vulnerability factor" as a kind of complement to this concept of recent life events as a significant precipitating factor. Brown proposed that individuals already under considerable duress sometimes experience a last straw or vulnerability factor that pushes them over the edge; for example, Brown researched poor women in the Camberwell district of London who were confined indoors with several children — the "last straw," then, would be that such women had no one to confide in or had lost a parent at an early age.

Some individuals with bipolar disease, the so-called "rapid-cyclers," apparently have such a strong genetic component for this illness that even the slightest stressful event can initiate an attack of depression or mania, but for others it might require a more significant life event coupled with the genetic vulnerability. We are susceptible to stress from any number of sources, but trauma that accompanies a period of significant change can be especially troublesome. For example, my own severe attacks occurred when I was a freshman in high school and, again, when I was a freshman in college. These are transition years in a young person's life; and in addition to the typical challenges of breaking into a high school and college routine, I had some added pressures: during my first year in high school my home environment was disturbed as my mother was away in a sanitarium fighting her way through a deep depression.

In my initial year in college I had difficulty finding that homeostasis, that proper balance with my environment Professor Whybrow talks about. I have found the routine of my adult years a definite asset in maintaining emotional stability; accordingly, during periods of transition and change such as my first year of college it is the lack of routine and certainty that make me vulnerable. As a freshman, I had no idea who I was or what I wanted from a college education. My father, both grandfathers, and two older brothers had all followed careers in business. As an eighteen-year-old I had no hint I would find my niche as a literature teacher.

My immediate goals for my freshman year at the University of Michigan were not particularly unrealistic: I sought to attain a B average in my studies, join a social fraternity, and make the Michigan tennis team. But dorm living, some poor decisions regarding academic course work, and a natural penchant for worry and anxiety led to a severe depression by semester's end.

Looking back I believe success was within my reach that freshman year. While it is true I selected courses that were clearly wrong for me (I chose engineering chemistry and later found my aptitude and interest in the humanities), my academic average remained salvageable. I had a reasonable shot at making the university's tennis team as I had been a high school state champion the previous spring. And, the fraternity of my choice had issued me a bid and I was enjoying my experience as a pledge. So I was well on the road to achieving my goals.

If I assess what destroyed my health in terms of what Brown has called the "vulnerability factor" in recent life events, I believe I would point to a bad habit I adopted that semester. I was never a particularly robust or energetic individual and when tennis practice, fraternity commitments, and academic demands began to mount, I started to tire. But I liked to spend late night hours writing and revising papers for my freshman composition class. To keep myself going, I started drinking large amounts of coffee.

Within just a short time, I found I was lying awake nights and could not sleep. Coffee can be the equivalent of a poison for one with this illness. The manic-depressive's neuroendocrine system is especially sensitive to a stimulant like caffeine: this chemical and the loss of sleep it promotes can lead to an onset of mania. Studies show serious depression can actually be lifted by inducing sleep loss. But, for a bipolar individual subject to severe mood swings, sleep deprivation can be very dangerous as it can induce mania and perhaps a phase of long and painful cycling. This was my experience as the insomnia contributed to an ever-increasing emotional disturbance and an inability to concentrate on daily assignments or to realize any degree of pleasure or fulfillment. I became increasingly concerned as my performance levels began falling off in all three sectors of my life: the academic, athletic, and social; but, the anxiety was also owing to the knowledge I'd had this illness four years earlier and the paralyzing fear I would have to be "locked away" someplace again and subjected to a frightening treatment.

It is worth comparing my situation to Brown's study of the women in the Camberwell section of London. These women were poor with too many children, but that vulnerability factor, that "last straw" that put them over the edge, was the lack of someone to confide

35

in. Dr. Dennis Murphy of the National Institute of Mental Health tells us that manic-depressives have a shortened form of a specific gene, 5-HTTP, making them less capable of processing the neurotransmitter, serotonin, and more susceptible to worry and anxiety. My tendency to tire easily, my new challenges as a college freshman, and this genetic propensity for worry represent the underlying causes for my breakdown, but that reckless consumption of coffee and the resulting loss of sleep might have provided the decisive catalyst or "last straw" effect Brown talks about.

The mania bottomed out in complete depression requiring the shock treatments at Mercywood. And, because my illness prevented my taking final exams for the first semester and required hospitalization well into the second, I lost the entire first year of college. The experience had been so devastating for me and I had lost so much in the way of self-confidence and self-esteem I opted not to return to Michigan. I remained in my home town and completed my first two years at a small liberal arts college there.

Partly because the University of Michigan provides a good education for the money and because I do not like to think of myself as a quitter, I returned to Ann Arbor my junior year and eventually earned both a bachelors and masters degree in English from Michigan. But of those three goals I had set out for myself my freshman year, I only achieved the academic. The social fraternities begin to lose their appeal for many college students once they reach their junior year; and, I decided at that point in my education to prepare myself for a profession and give up my earlier dream to play major college tennis.

The experts seem to agree that transition years can be especially taxing on individuals subject to manic depression. Kay Jamison, Ph.D., qualified in the previous chapter, lectures college administrators, faculty, and especially students across the country on the high risk to freshmen for deep depression and suicide because of all the change and pressure consistent with that first year of college. Change also seems a factor in the large numbers of women who experience mental illness. Instability is most common, for instance, following child birth or divorce. Change for women during a pregnancy and change for myself as a teenager was not, of course, restricted to external pressures; we were both subject to glandular upheaval at such times as well.

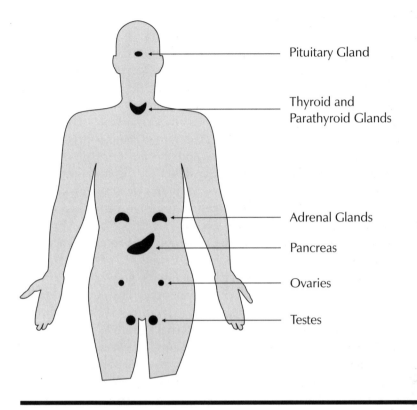

Pituitary Gland

Thyroid and
Parathyroid Glands

Adrenal Glands

Pancreas

Ovaries

Testes

Figure 4-2. The Endocrine System

The Endocrine System Provides a Key

For the most part, Selye's contributions centered on the endocrine system (see fig. 4-2), associated organs and tissues of the body that collectively release substances known as hormones. Endocrine organs are known also as ductless glands because their hormone secretions are released directly into the bloodstream. Technically, those glands that comprise the endocrine system are the pituitary, adrenal, thyroid, parathyroid, ovaries, testes, pancreas, and placenta. The kidney, liver, pineal body, gastrointestinal tract, upper intestine and heart also secrete a part of this mix of chemical substances that involve the endocrine system. It is this system which includes the stress, energy, sexual, and rhythmic messenger systems of the body — the steroid, thyroid, gonadal, and pineal hormones respectively. Science has found it is these hormonal systems that are typically disordered in mood disturbance (Whybrow 1997).

Endocrine function is regulated also by the nervous system as the different endocrine organs are brought under nervous control in a variety of ways. The adrenal medulla and the posterior pituitary are richly innervated glands directly controlled by the nervous system. The adrenal cortex, thyroid, and gonads, however, although responding to various nervous stimuli, have no apparent nerve supply and continue to function when transplanted to other parts of the body. The anterior pituitary has a scanty nerve supply but cannot function if transplanted.

With his general adaptation syndrome, Selye was able to trace the series of chemical changes characteristic of this neuroendocrine system when besieged by stress. From the time of Selye's breakthroughs there could be little doubt that this system of nerve stimuli and endocrinal secretions feels the greatest impact when psychological or physical stress confronts man. Selye learned that at the onset of uncommon stress, a tiny gland at the base of the brain, the pituitary — the boss of the body's repair crew — starts protective action by secreting chemical messengers, or hormones, ACTH or STH. These hormones, carried in the blood to two small glands above the kidneys, the adrenals, cause the outside border of these glands, or cortex, to produce cortisone and other messengers (see Figure 4-3). Although the center of these glands manufacture adrenaline, the adrenal hormones in question are those made by the cortex.

The adrenal cortex hormones quickly prepare the body — along with various other chemical changes involving the body's proteins and sugars — for fight or flight. These changes also make it possible to repair vital tissues by a process of robbing Peter to pay Paul. This stage called the "Alarm Reaction" varies in intensity with the degree of stress.

If trauma continues the body sets up a "Stage of Resistance" in which it repairs itself by rebuilding with all the raw material at hand. These first two stages of G.A.S. , "Alarm" and "Resistance," are char-

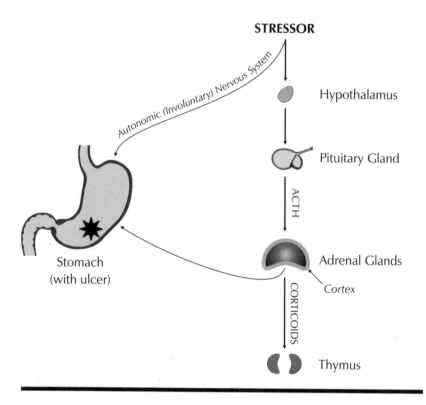

STRESSOR

Autonomic (Involuntary) Nervous System

Hypothalamus

Pituitary Gland

ACTH

Stomach
(with ulcer)

Adrenal Glands

Cortex

CORTICOIDS

Thymus

Figure 4-3. Principal Pathways Mediating
the Response to a Stressor

acterized by constant damage and repair; most illnesses fall in stage three, "Exhaustion."

Selye's stress theory had important implications for all of medicine, but its relevance for bipolar disorder is especially significant. The major contribution of G.A.S. is the concept of non-specificity; that is to say, any event that causes conflict, tension, or trauma for the body, psychological or physical, will create the same chain of chemical and hormonal secretions and the identical three stage process from alarm through resistance to exhaustion. Selye knew the ductless glands of the endocrine system (the pituitary, adrenals, hypothalamus, pineal, etc.) that secrete the hormonal changes consistent with his stress reaction theory could lead to mental and emotional disturbance.

Researchers specializing in manic-depressive illness validate Selye's theories. Manic depression is now considered a biologic disease and of those studies attempting to trace the chemical changes in the body to prove its physiological basis, the most respected strongly implicate the endocrine system. These studies show an excess of the hormone, cortisol, in over 50 per cent of depressed patients tested. (Sachar, 1982). Cortisol is one of the hormones secreted by the endocrines observed in Selye's G.A.S., and the 50 per cent figure cited in Sachar's study would likely have been even higher had the patients included in his study been screened to include just those with primarily endogenic disease (emotional illness resulting from disturbed body chemistry as opposed to depression that emanates more exclusively from neurosis). An elevated cortisol level in the blood is especially significant because it is not only a sign of the human organism under stress but also figures importantly in the symptoms of the disease. "Hormones, particularly the stress hormones of cortisol and thyroxin, and the sex steroids, help determine the limbic brain's homeostatic set point. Any rapid change in these hormone levels, therefore, demands immediate accommodation, and while adaptation is proceeding, mood is commonly unstable" (Whybrow 1997).

Actually, cortisol represents the hormonal end point of hypothalmic-pituitary-adrenal (HPA) activity. When an individual experiences stress, the major force driving excessive cortisol production (see Figure 4-4) is increased hypothalamic secretion of CRF (Corticotropin Releasing Factor), which stimulates ACTH secretion from the anterior pituitary into the peripheral circulation. The latter hormone activates production and release of cortisol and other corticosteroids from the adrenocortical gland.

The Disease Mechanisms

If Selye's general adaptation syndrome and the chemical changes experienced in a manic-depressive when undergoing an attack actually travel the identical HPA axis pathways, we are naturally curious as to any difference in the two. Selye's syndrome is a universal principle

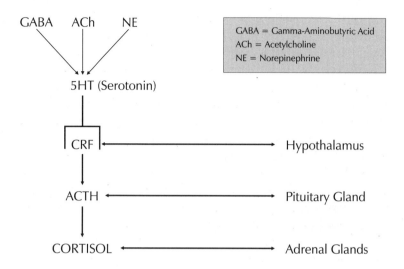

When triggered by a stressor, CRF (corticotropin-releasing factor) from the hypothalamus in the brain causes a release of the hormone ACTH from the pituitary gland which in turn serves as a catalyst for the release of the hormone cortisol from the adrenal cortex.

5-HT (serotonin) seems to function as a quarterback for a team of neurotransmitters and neuropeptides that control the CRF. If 5-HT is readily available to the brain, the individual handles stress normally. If there is insufficient 5-HT, there is a resulting hypersecretion of ACTH from the pituitary and uncontrolled cortisol from the adrenal cortex — and the symptoms of bipolar disease.

Figure 4-4. The HPA Axis: Neurotransmitter Control of Corticotropin-Releasing Factor Secretion

and occurs in all of us, normal or sick, when confronted with a physical or psychological stressor. For a healthy person experiencing a stressor there will be elevated counts of the hormones ACTH and cortisol as a normal part of their internal mechanism to match external stressor demands. Among these healthy individuals once the exposure to a stressor has passed, the stress hormone levels of ACTH and cortisol return to a normal level of output. For persons prone to bipolar disorder, however, the secretion of these hormones continues though the exposure to the stressor is long over. So one very fundamental way for individuals with bipolar disorder to understand the cause of their illness is to appreciate the defective nature of their endocrine system. A taxing job, an unhappy marriage, another illness (psychological or physical), any kind of life maladjustment can be the stressor to trigger an attack of this disease. (See Appendix C for a list of physical illnesses that can contribute to manic depression or mimic its symptoms).

Neurotransmitters Fail Bipolars

The exaggerated secretion of cortisol observed in manic-depressives under stress is thought to be related to an abnormality linked to the hypothalamus and the pituitary gland. (Holsboer, 1983 & Holsboer et al. 1984, 1988). The reason for this increased production of cortisol and the hyperactive pituitary gland appears to involve the brain's neurotransmitters — those chemicals that comprise the brain's messenger system. Several major neurotransmitter systems (serotonin, noradrenaline, dopamine, acetylcholine, etc.) have been implicated in the regulation of CRF (corticotropin-releasing factor) from the paraventricular nucleus of the hypothalamus. But the role of these neurotransmitter systems in this specific CRF release and in their more general impact on mood states is enormously complex. Originally, for instance, it was believed insufficient amounts of these neurotransmitters could produce depression while excessive amounts caused mania or elated moods. That theory still holds some credence, but as science has achieved increased understanding over the past several years we now know these neurotransmitter systems impact one another, work in unison with the neuropeptides, and that pre- and post synaptic receptors and the interaction of receptors with second and third messenger systems all play a vital role in this intricate process.

"The changing blood flow patterns that brain imaging reveals during mood disorder and in recovery presumably reflects a limbic fermentation and disorganization of neurotransmitter activity. The usually precise interchange of messages that sustains communication

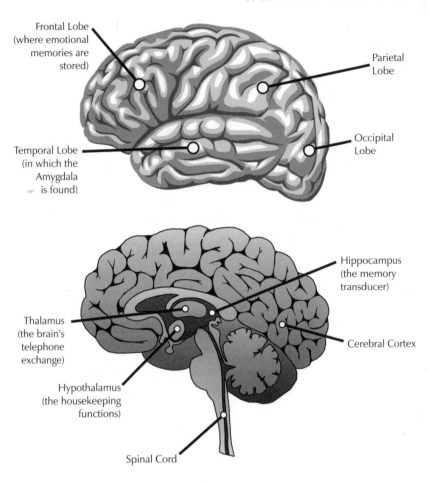

Frontal Lobe
(where emotional
memories are
stored)

Parietal
Lobe

Temporal Lobe
(in which the
Amygdala
is found)

Occipital
Lobe

Hippocampus
(the memory
transducer)

Thalamus
(the brain's
telephone
exchange)

Cerebral Cortex

Hypothalamus
(the housekeeping
functions)

Spinal Cord

**Figure 4-5. The Limbic Alliance
(the emotional center of the brain)**

among the thalamus, hippocampus, amygdala, and the frontal cortex
of the limbic alliance (see fig. 4-5) is disturbed. New information from
the environment is no longer attended to or processed swiftly by the
thalamus, and the emotional memory banks of the frontal lobe churn

without purpose, as the true emotional significance of ongoing events becomes blurred by the preoccupation with remembrance. The homeostatic systems of the emotional brain have adopted a new steady state, one less responsive to the environment and less adaptive" (Whybrow 1997).

Serotonin (5-HT) the Most Promising

Of the several neurotransmitter systems, serotonin (also known as 5 hydroxytryptamine or 5-HT) has been the most intensively studied in relation to the biology of depression and the mechanism of antidepressant action. The emphasis on 5-HT has been maintained primarily because of results from studies investigating the mechanism of antidepressant action (Heninger & Charney 1987). The most intriguing of these studies have been electrophysiological tests in laboratory animals suggesting that most antidepressant drugs and electroconvulsive therapy enhance neurotransmission across serotonin (5-HT) synapses after long term but not short term administration (de Montigny & Blier 1984, Fuxe et al 1984, Blier et al 1990a). Biochemists hypothesize that 5-HT provides long-term as opposed to immediate relief because, as we suggest above, in spite of its obvious centrality in mood shifts it apparently works in unison with another system or systems. This delay in relief can also be attributed to the "Neurotransmitter Receptor Hypothesis of Depression," a theory that says depression is caused by faulty receptors and while antidepressants *immediately* boost monoamine neurotransmitters it takes a period of time (sometimes weeks) before these monoamines can alter the receptors (see Figures 6.2-6.5). While according to this hypothesis flawed receptors cause the depression, it is also believed that the depletion of monoamine neurotransmitters (like serotonin) disturb the receptors in the first place.

The "Permissive Hypothesis"

So while other neurotransmitter systems, neuropeptides, synaptic receptors, etc. all play a role in an attack of bipolar disorder, serotonin appears the major player in this complex synthesis of chemicals. Various preclinical studies in laboratory animals demonstrate serotonin (this 5-HT system) is involved in the regulation of many of the types of physiological processes which form the core symptoms of depression. The behaviors regulated by the 5-HT system in laboratory animals include a wide variety of these physiological processes including appetite, sexual function, pain sensitivity, body temperature, and circadian (sleep) rhythms (Meltzer & Lowry 1987). Overall, serotonin plays a critical role in the central nervous system. When this neurotransmitter is in short supply, it is associated with a change in a wide variety of behaviors. According to what has been called the "permissive hypothesis" of serotonin, both the manic and the depressive phases of bipolar illness are characterized by an undersupply of this neurotransmitter. Extensive data from a variety of animal species suggest that brain serotonin systems dampen or inhibit a variety of functions influenced by other neurotransmitters. The permissive hypothesis postulates that defective serotonin inhibiting of other neurotransmitter systems (perhaps especially the norepinephrine and dopamine systems) permits the wide excursion between depression and mania. To this extent, the original hypothesis of too much/ too little remains credible — but with a twist. Too little 5-HT seems to be implicated in emotional swings in both directions, highs and lows.

Bipolars Lack 5-HT

Meltzer and colleagues (1984) administered serotonin orally to depressed patients and controls and measured changes in serum cortisol. Previous studies in both laboratory animals and humans had implicated central serotonin systems in the regulation of ACTH and cortisol secretion, presumably through regulation of hypothalamic CRF release (Fuller, 1981). This oral administration of serotonin performed by Meltzer induced a significantly greater increase in serum cortisol in depressed patients than in controls (Meltzer et al, 1984). Of special interest, this supersensitive response, presumably reflecting decreased serotonin activity, was more pronounced in the bipolar than in the unipolar depressed patients and also was observed in manic patients. Since elevated cortisol levels are a sign of stress and the administration of serotonin should correct and not exacerbate the condition, we are surprised when cortisol continues up. The answer is in the serotonin receptors that are "upregulated," disturbed, and react supersensitively to the administration of the serotonin, thus sending the stress indicator, cortisol, up. After a period of time, the increased serotonin neurotransmitters will "downregulate" the serotonin receptors, desensitizing them, returning them to a normal state — and the cortisol (stress) level will drop.

There was no significant difference in response during the depression or mania. In related studies (Meltzer et al, 1984), the exaggerated cortisol response to serotonin was shown to be positively correlated with both depressive and manic symptoms, significantly greater in psychotic and in suicidal patients, and, interestingly, significantly more variable in bipolar than unipolar patients, suggesting perhaps greater instability of this system in bipolar illness.

Lithium and Tryptophan Affect Serotonin

The results of these studies, therefore, seem to indicate that bipolar (and some unipolar) patients may have decreased central serotonin activity, resulting in serotonin receptors that are more sensitive (and perhaps less stable). Further, this abnormality seems to occur during both depression and mania. Such data are compatible with the hypothesis of Prange and co-workers (1974) and of Kety (1971) that a decrease in serotonin activity plays a permissive role in the pathogenesis of both depression and mania. Along with these findings related to decreased serotonin activity is the interesting discovery that the effective use of lithium in manic-depressives is associated with a marked increase in the serotonin-induced secretion of cortisol (Meltzer et al., 1984). This discovery substantiates another finding that lithium facilitates serotonin activity in animals. Moreover, consistent with the permissive hypothesis are findings suggesting on-going lithium use enhances or stabilizes central serotonin systems (Mandell and Knapp, 1979), as well as clinical reports of successful preventative action when lithium is used in conjunction with precursors for serotonin, such as the amino acid, tryptophan.

A Summary

Our discussion, then, of serotonin as one of the major neurotransmitter systems clearly suggests a link between the neurotransmitters and the hypothalmic secretions characteristic of stress. While all of us experience Selye's general adaptation syndrome in response to stress, it would seem indivduals with bipolar disorder have a flaw in this stress response system involving the neurotransmitters. We have seen, for example, that the latest antidepressants (the selective serotonin reuptake inhibitors) and lithium apparently work so universally on manic-depressives because they markedly increase serotonin activity. We will subsequently show (see chapters 5 & 6) that the serotonin levels, and the levels of the other neurotransmitters involved in the neuroendocrine system and in the body's reaction to stress, can be enhanced with drugs like the SSRIs and lithium but also through diet, amino acids, and vitamins.

Stress, Serotonin Levels, and Sleep

The insufficient serotonin activity that accounts for an individual's inability to combat stress, and, indeed allows for a "permissive role" in the pathogenesis of both depression and mania could also contribute significantly to sleep problems so characteristic of manic-depressives. Decreased serotonin activity might account for the reduced amount of sleep time spent in the REM (rapid-eye-movement) period (Born, et al 1987). While low serotonin levels and stress-induced cortisol tend to reduce REM sleep and increase slow wave (NREM) sleep, other hypothalamic-pituitary-adrenal axis peptide hormones tend to counteract part of this process by reducing slow wave sleep time as well. The net effect, then, of bipolars under stress is to experience a reduction in both modes of sleep, REM and NREM.

The Neuroendocrine System

The neurotransmitters, such as serotonin, and the hormone secretions of the hypothalamic axis are not only involved in sleep disruption but also figure significantly in controlling emotional activity, body temperature, thirst, hunger, water balance, and sexual function. If we look

47

back to chapter 3 and visit the list of symptoms for severe depression and/or mania, we find problems that involve these same functions. We simply cannot overestimate the role of stress, the hormonal activity of the hypothalamic-pituitary-adrenal axis, and the neurotransmitters in bipolar disease.

5 Nutrition's Vital Role

"This is my letter to the world
That never wrote to me —
The simple news that Nature told
With tender majesty.

Her message is committed
To hands I cannot see;
For love of her, sweet countrymen,
Judge tenderly of me!"

— Emily Dickinson

One way to preempt the third stage, exhaustion, in Selye's general adaptation syndrome is to avoid frustration and other kinds of destructive stress; another means, however, of maintaining homeostasis and health is to shore up those raw materials the body draws upon when besieged by stress. We have shown the endocrine system and most specifically the pituitary, adrenal, and hypothalamus glands are implicated in the body's response to stress; and, we have observed that

49

the endocrine system in individuals with bipolar disorder seems flawed by an inability to consistently produce the required amount of the neurotransmitters. There are nutritional measures we can take to fortify the pertinent glands of the endocrine system and insure the amino acids and vitamins necessary for the production of neurotransmitters.

The pharmaceutical companies are spending billions in research to best their competition in mass-producing vital neurotransmitters like serotonin, and I tell you in the previous paragraph we can do that with proper diet and vitamin supplements. Such a claim might induce you to stop reading this "foolishness" and put the book down. Please be patient and read on. What you learn here will prove extremely valuable; and, I will not be doing anything so radical as to recommend you throw out your drugs. But you do need to appreciate that we can metabolize at least a portion of the serotonin we need with an amino acid, tryptophan (a protein, that exists in many of our foods), and vitamin B-complex. Evidence also suggests we can significantly diminish side effects of psychiatric drugs through diet and megadoses of the vitamin supplements.

I fully understand the skepticism. When we think "cure" or "restoration of health" in this society we think doctors, hospitals, surgical wards, and drugs. We do not think foods and vitamins. And, typically, we will not be apprised of the benefits inherent in nutrition from our primary care physicians, the M.D.'s or the D.O.'s. Over the past decade or two, some medical schools have started to lecture in complementary medicines, such as nutrition. But these lectures are often voluntary, and our young doctors still do not receive the background in nutritional science they need.

I personally stumbled on the value of nutrition quite by chance. I was home from college for the summer a year or two after that second severe attack I describe in chapters 1 and 4. For summer work I was painting houses and when that was slow I mowed lawns. One of my lawn jobs sent me to the home of an elderly aunt. My aunt, actually my mother's aunt, my great aunt, was well into her eighties at the time. She conversed with my mother regularly and knew of my history of manic depression, and one afternoon while fixing me a cold drink during a break from the lawn work she opined that I might do well to take a fist full of Brewer's Yeast tablets twice a day.

I had never heard of Brewer's Yeast and knew next to nothing about nutrition or vitamins. But my elderly aunt was still able to manage the farm property she and her deceased husband had owned for over fifty years; and, in addition to the sinewy, tough, and able older woman I could see before me I recalled stories my mother had passed on to me for many years. My aunt never had children of her own, but her own mother had died very young and she, the oldest, had to fill in as mother to several younger siblings. Later, as a married woman, she not only helped her husband operate the farm, but she also managed a local office of the Pittsburgh Plate Glass company for forty years. When this lady with such an impressive background and still a twinkle in her eye and sturdy gate at 85 suggested I might benefit from Brewer's Yeast tablets, I was inclined to listen. My aunt had such credibility with me that I went to the health food store later that day and started the tablets the next morning. I have never looked back in over thirty-five years. Moreover, I have never had an attack with anything near the severity of those two I had prior to starting the tablets.

Because I have initiated any number of strategies to diminish the potential for a severe attack following that second one at eighteen, it is highly improbable my aunt's recommendation is the sole reason for my good fortune. Still there might be something to it. In the years following her advice, I have made a very thorough investigation of nutritional science. If I have read one book on nutrition, I have read 50. My interest in the value of nutritional science was fully launched in my mid-twenties when my mother-in-law introduced me to the books of the internationally known nutritionist, Adelle Davis. Davis had a wonderful background in biochemistry and nutritional studies at the University of California at Berkeley, Purdue University, and did postgraduate work at Columbia University. Because of this academic background Davis, more than any other, placed nutritional science on a sound footing; and, at least two of her works are still in print twenty-five years after her death.

One of the facts I have uncovered in my study is that Brewer's Yeast tablets contain both protein and B-complex vitamins. As nutritional research has become increasingly sophisticated and respected over the course of the last half-century — and growing increasingly so with each passing year — the studies consistently recommend the B vitamins for illness involving the nervous system and emotions. With all the recent attention given the neurotransmitter, serotonin, it is even more remarkable that my aunt's Brewer's Yeast supplied the B-complex to help my body metabolize the amino acid, tryptophan, naturally occurring in my foods into that precious neurotransmitter.

Nutrition Specific to the Endocrines

Contemporary man's susceptability to allergies, stomach ulcers, arthritis, nephritis, and countless other diseases, including depression, suggests the importance of the endocrine glands to the preservation of health. The millions who suffer from "stress diseases" and the enormous number of maladies for which cortisone is now given as a treatment indicate the significant numbers who suffer from adrenal exhaustion. To meet the demands of stress, according to Adelle Davis, ". . . the starting point is to obtain all nutrients necessary for the production of the pituitary and adrenal hormones. Of these, the quantities of protein, vitamine C, and B-complex vitamins required are particularly large, but they vary with individuals and the severity of stress."

The Nerves Demand Protein

The protein Davis calls for as a response to stress is the primary substance of the body after water. It is composed of amino acids sometimes referred to as the "building blocks" of life. These amino acids consist of 16 per cent nitrogen and this determines their difference from carbohydrates and fats in the body. Twenty-nine well known amino acids make up the hundreds of different types of protein present in all living things. In our bodies, the liver produces roughly 80 percent of the amino acids required. The other 20 percent must come from outside our bodies. To gain what we call a "complete protein," it must include all of its particular amino acids. The amino acids, however, can be linked together to near infinity as they can form more than 50,000 separate proteins and 20,000 different enzymes. Since each type of protein is made of different amino acids, each designed to meet a different need, the various proteins are not interchangeable. Those amino acids needed by our bodies to produce complete proteins but only available externally through diet are known as the "essential amino acids." These are arginine, histidine, isoleucine, leucine, lysine, methionine, phenylalanine, threonine, tryptophan, and valine. Other amino acids making up the 20 percent not available from the liver but those the body seems to gain from sources other than diet are: alanine, arginine, aspartic acid, asparagine, glutamic acid, glutamine, glycine, proline, and serine.

Proteins and their amino acids are the virtual equivalent of the life force itself. Nutritionists are especially concerned we shore up our proteins to combat stress because the central nervous system simply cannot do its job without amino acids. The amino acids perform as neurotransmitters or as precursors to the neurotransmitters. In other words, the brain does not receive and send messages with neurotransmitters, without amino acids. Unless all of the amino acids required are available to the brain, almost any breakdown can occur in the transmission of a message. Proteins and their amino acids are so vital to the proper functioning of the brain one meal high in protein will temporarily increase alertness.

Nutrition Linked to Moods

This causal relation between the brain's behavior and food is becoming increasingly evident. Mood swings in the direction of mania or depression can most often be linked to stress or to stress in some combination with diet — with poor eating habits and junk foods. The brain's neurotransmitters, which govern our behaviorial tendencies, are clearly influenced by what we eat. The major neurotransmitters are serotonin, dopamine, and norepinephrine. If the brain is healthy in its production of serotonin, it has a greater capacity to cope with stress and reduce tension. Moreover, if the brain is producing dopamine and norepinephrine in ample supply, we can act and think more readily and we tend to be appreciably more alert.

If we eat wisely, then, and with generally sound judgment, we will produce the neurotransmitters that decidely govern our moods and emotional and mental health. In general, complex carbohydrates — raw fruits and vegetables — will have a calming effect on us; protein meals including fatty acids and/or carbohydrates will tend to make us more alert and energetic. Salmon, white fish, and turkey are all smart choices for the manic-depressive or depressive. Conversely, anyone suffering from an emotional disorder or fatigue should clearly avoid pork, the fried foods, hamburgers — the typical junk food. The fats in these foods are known to prevent the synthesis of neurotransmitters by the brain and encourage the blood cells to adhere and clump, preventing good circulation — especially to the brain (Balch 1990).

So diet for the manic-depressive should consist of vegetables, fruits, nuts, seeds, beans, and legumes. Whole grains are recommended, but it is not wise to consume inordinate amounts of bread. We should try to eat whitefish, salmon, and turkey twice a week. The diet itself must be the cornerstone for our nutritional response to stress and manic-depressive disease. When we consider the complexity of the chemical combinations constituting the proteins, amino acids, and their enzymes, we are humbled by this magical biochemistry inherent in our own bodies. We must first, therefore, ensure a balance in what we eat. On the other hand, when disease appears to invade our bodies because of the malabsorption or improper synthesis of certain foods and their nutrients, a strong case can be made for supplementing a balanced diet with specific vitamins, amino acids, minerals, and herbs. We found in chapter 4, for example, that serotonin is a neurotransmitter pivotal in responding to stress and because serotonin is dependent upon the amino acid tryptophan for its production, this is a nutrient manic-depressives should consciously supplement in their diets. Melatonin, a natural hormone and close cousin to tryptophan and serotonin molecularly, and St. John's Wort (Hypericum perforatum), a natural herb, also show potential as nutritional supplements beneficial to those subject to mood swing. We will consider melatonin and St. John's Wort in our discussion of nutrition and the mood stabilizers in Chapter 6.

5-HTP Provides Alternative to Tryptophan

For over thirty years isolated tryptophan was readily available to us in capsule form; the nutrient was used as a dietary supplement to treat depression, insomnia, premenstrual syndrome, stress, and hyperactivity in children. Unfortunately, this is no longer the case. In December of 1989 the Federal Drug Administration (FDA) took tryptophan off the market because of the outbreak of a rare blood disorder among some individuals who were taking this substance. The blood disorder, eosinophilia-myalgia syndrome (EMS), was linked to impurities in the supplements as well as immune system weaknesses which enhanced susceptibility to the illness. Of 1,550 known cases in the United States as of May 1990, 24 deaths were reported.

The outbreak of EMS was vigorously investigated and responsible research traces the problem to a contaminated batch of tryptophan produced by one Japanese manufacturer. Despite the fact that the FDA and the Centers for Disease Control and Prevention have both concluded that virtually all EMS patients used tryptophan from the Showa Denko K.K. company of Japan, this amino acid continues to be banned in capsules or tablets. There are currently two alternatives, however, for obtaining tryptophan in tablet form. It is available through prescription from your doctor and many of the health food stores have available a product called 5-HTP which has been developed to side-step the FDA ruling and is purported to have the same effect and benefits of the original tryptophan (Goldberg 1993).

Wurtman Research Significant

In addition to this understanding that 5-HTP is currently available as a supplement, we need to be aware of the work of Richard Wurtman. As a medical doctor and director of MIT's Clinical Research Center, Wurtman has made important discoveries concerning the most effective ways to absorb tryptophan in our food consumption. Reporting on the work of her husband in her book, *The Serotonin Solution,* Judith Wurtman tells us tryptophan enters the brain more quickly and in greater quantities when we are eating carbohydrates. This is contrary to our expectations since tryptophan is an amino acid, a protein; but, Richard Wurtman and a graduate assistant, John Fernstrom, found that tryptophan shaped like so many other amino acids competes with these other proteins for space to enter the brain; and, therefore, gains greater access to the brain fluids when the body is consuming carbohydrates — not proteins.

In conducting their research on rats, Wurtman and Fernstrom

found that tryptophan is at a disadvantage in gaining brain access because it tends to be found in lesser amounts in protein than all the other amino acids. The scientists found the human brain can realize an appreciable gain in its amounts of tryptophan and serotonin while consuming carbohydrates because of the activity of insulin, a hormone secreted by the pancreas whenever we eat carbohydrates. Once we digest carbohydrates, insulin enters the bloodstream and pushes glucose, the digested form of carbohydrates, into the cells where it is used for energy. During this process insulin also pushes amino acids circulating in the blood into the muscle cells. For reasons not fully understood, insulin leaves tryptophan behind in the bloodstream, where it is now free to enter the brain unimpeded by competition from other amino acids.

So, while it is clearly advantageous for manic-depressives to eat significant quantities of tryptophan and thereby manufacture high levels of serotonin, that goal presents some unique considerations regarding diet. Turkey and white fish are known to contain large quantities of tryptophan, but Wurtman's insightful research tells us merely eating increased amounts of those foods is no guarantee we will realize the desired tryptophan; we need to balance the consumption of these protein foods with carbohydrates and properly time the intake of these two major food groups to allow the tryptophan to pass into the brain (See Appendix A). In the following section we learn that tryptophan levels can be increased by ingesting large doses of specific vitamins as well as by our intake of specific foods.

Megavitamin Therapy

Megavitamin therapy takes its name from the root "mega," meaning large or of great size. If one adopts the megavitamin theory, a daily dose of vitamin C might comprise 1 to 5 grams as opposed to the more typical 100 to 500 mgs. This practice of using larger doses of vitamins to treat health problems is known as orthomolecular medicine. Dr. Abram Hoffer (former director of psychiatric research, University Hospital, Saskatoon, Saskatchewan) and Dr. Humphrey Osmond (New Jersey Neuro-Psychiatric Institute, Princeton, New Jersey), and the better known two-time Nobel prize winner for chemistry, Dr.

Linus Pauling have all pioneered and championed the practice of orthomolecular psychiatry. Pauling is actually credited with originating the term "orthomolecular" to suggest an approach to medicine that utilizes naturally occuring substances normally present in the body. The prefix "ortho" means normal or correct, and orthomolecular physicians believe in a great many instances physiological and psychological disorders can be corrected through the proper adjustment and balance of amino acids, vitamins, minerals, and other similar substances in the body.

Psychiatry and Nutrition

Drs. Hoffer, Osmond, and Pauling have achieved remarkable success working from the assumption that mental and emotional disorders are nutritional problems, triggered by a stress or shock that requires more than the body's reserves to handle. These orthomolecular doctors contend those treating emotional disturbance must also diagnose and treat the nutritional or genetic deficiency. The orthomolecular approach knows very well there is an on-going need for the more traditional treatments of psychiatrists and psychotherapists, but it contends traditional psychiatry could be at least twice as effective if genetic and nutritional deficiencies were met.

We can show proof that emotional and mental disease has a biochemical basis. Symptoms will appear and disappear even as we administer and withdraw megavitamin therapy — and we can observe these changes when the patient has no knowledge of any alterations in the treatment. Science is finding many of the emotionally and mentally ill are lacking in one or more of the B-complex vitamins or vitamin C. British physician Dr. R. Shulman revealed in the 1967 British Journal of Psychiatry that 48 of 59 psychiatric cases had folic acid (one of the B-complex vitamins) deficiencies. Also, Dr. F. Lucksch, a German psychiatrist, stated in Wien Klin Wochenschr, 1940, that 75 percent of his patients suffered from vitamin C deficiencies. Dr. Lucksch found that giving these patients mega doses of vitamin C improved two-thirds of them (Passwater 1977).

Additional evidence points to a biochemical basis for mental and emotional disease: (1) mental disorders are frequently genetic — as we have seen in manic-depressive illness; (2) samples of patient's urine clearly reveal chemical abnormalities; (3) the physical changes that sometimes accompany the disease, and (4) a perfectly healthy person, psychologically, can be made to mimic the symptoms of emotional disturbance through the use of chemicals. All four of these reasons strongly suggest it is inadvisable to treat mental illness as solely a psychological disorder. Moreover, people otherwise normal will begin to exhibit symptoms of depression and other evidence of mental disturbance when they are lacking in folic acid or niacin (both of which constitute part of the B-complex vitamins).

Special Need for B Vitamins

The B vitamins exist in nature as a family of similar chemical properties. Any substance ingested in the body must be taken with reason and care, but the B-vitamins are relatively safe to take in mega or large doses because they are water-soluble and the human body will take what it needs of the vitamins and eliminate the remainder. Those who have realized great success treating nutritional deficiencies and genetic defects with megavitamin therapy know the old medical-school/ traditional medicine adage that claims consuming extra vitamins is like trying to pour more coffee into a full cup is wrong. In the body, the cup is never full; although some spills over, more is used.

The B-complex group includes thiamine(B-1), riboflavin(B-2), niacin (B-3, also known as niacinamide or nicotinic acid), pantothenic acid (B-5), pyridoxine (B-6), cyanocobalamin (B-12), pangamic acid (B-15), amygdalin (B-17), lipoic acid (or thioctic acid), biotin (H), folic acid (Bc or M), inositol, p-aminobenzoic acid (PABA), choline, and other, still unisolated vitamins. Choline is the only vitamin of the B-complex family that does not function as a coenzyme.

A coenzyme is a segment of an enzyme, an extensive molecule which serves to spark or trigger chemical reactions in the body. Without enzymes, the chemical processes in the human body would proceed much too slowly to sustain life. The enzymes actually consist of two major divisions: the apoenzyme and the coenzyme. The apoenzyme provides the protein portion of the chemical and the coenzyme the nonprotein section. Niacinamide (B-3) is typically administered in large doses in megavitamin therapy. B-3 forms two significant coenzymes, nicotinamide adenine dinucleotide (NAD) and nicotinamide adenine dinucleotide phosphate (NADP). These NAD and NADP coenzymes function importantly in more than fifty different enzymes. NAD and NADP are believed responsible for metabolizing carbohydrates (especially sugars), fats, and proteins. Without sufficient amounts of NAD and NADP, these normal nutrients — especially the amino acid tryptophan — end up as poisons in the blood since they have been improperly metabolized. Tryptophan, as we show above, can form serotonin. Serotonin is the neurotransmitter that received so much attention in our earlier discussion of the neuroendocrine system and Hans Selye's theories on stress.

The causal link posited here from the coenzymatic action of the B-complex vitamins to metabolizing the amino acid, tryptophan, and then the neurotransmitter, serotonin, is of significance. Some doctors, nutritionists, and various medical practitioners have suggested for some time that individuals with bipolar disorder appear to have difficulty with the absorption and proper synthesis of the B-complex vitamins (Balch 1990). Just above we have learned of the link from the B vitamins to tryptophan and serotonin. The argument that the B-complex vitamins can figure importantly in improving emotional and mental health, therefore, gains a great deal of credence. This link with serotonin gains more support when we recall our earlier observation that lithium is believed to work effectively with manic-depressives because it is thought to increase the activity of this same neurotransmitter.

Must Consider Individual Needs

We must remember not only the unique complexity of our chemical makeup, but also that our individual needs for supplements vary significantly according to our diet and the degree of stress we experience at any one time. It is, therefore, difficult to be precise in recommending vitamin supplements, but in their book *Prescription for Nutritional Healing*, James F. Balch, M.D. and Phyllis A. Balch, C.N.C., suggest the following dosages for those diagnosed with bipolar disease.

Nutrients

SUPPLEMENT	SUGGESTED DOSAGE	COMMENTS
Very Important		
L-taurine (amino acid)	500 mg 3 times daily. Take with 50 mg vitamin B-6 and 100 mg vitamin C for better absorption.	L-taurine deficiency results in hyperactivity, anxiety, and poor brain function.
L-Tyrosine (amino acid)	500 mg twice daily on an empty stomach. Add a small amount of vitamins B-6 and C for better assimilation.	Important in treating depression. Stabilizes mood swings.
Protein (free form amino acids)	Twice daily on an empty stomach.	Needed for normal brain function. Combats depression.
Vitamin B complex or liver injections and	2 cc twice a week.	These all can be taken in one injection. The B vitamins are essential for normal brain function.
vitamin B-12 and vitamin B-6 (pyridoxine) or	one-half cc twice a week.	
vitamin B complex (hypoallergenic) capsules or tablets with	100 mg 3 times daily	
B-12 lozenges	1 tablet twice daily on an empty stomach.	Important in making myelin, the sheath covering the nerves.
Zinc	50 mg daily.	Protects the brain cells.

Lithium	By prescription only	Alters the manic-depressive cycles, producing mood stability.

Helpful

Multivitamin and mineral complex (high potency) containing	As directed on label.	Mineral imbalance may cause depression.
calcium and	1,500 mg	
magnesium	750 mg	

Unsaturated fatty acids	As directed on label.	

Vitamin C	3,000-6,000 mg (Take Ester C when possible)	A powerful immuno-stimulant. Aids allergic defenses.

In the *Nutrition Almanac* (4th ed.), Gayla and John Kirschmann make similar recommendations; however, they also suggest 750 mg daily of GABA, 300 mcg daily of chromium, and up to 100 mg of 5-HTP on an empty stomach. It seems reasonable to begin a supplement program by following these dosages suggested by the Balch and Kirschmann books. If these supplement amounts recommended by Balch and Kirschmann do not seem to improve the condition when taken on a consistent basis for 12 to 15 weeks, consider increasing the amounts — but always under the supervision of a physician.

Finding a Physician

If just beginning to assess the body's resilience to stress, its general condition, and possible need for better diet and/or vitamin and mineral supplementation, it might be wise to schedule an examination with your physician. However, an analysis to determine the body's nutritional condition can result in a surprising realization: most of mainstream, traditional medicine is poorly prepared to assist us in nutritional science. We assume our doctors are well informed in nutrition: in foods, vitamins, and minerals and their role in maintaining health and preventing disease; unfortunately, this is rarely the case. When we make an appointment with our family physician or internist, our M.D. or D.O., the first thing they want to know is what is wrong with us, where do we hurt. These doctors are perplexed if we wish to consult with them about health, how to maintain it, and how to prevent disease. They have been trained in how to cure and treat disease but not how to prevent it, and very few medical schools spend time teaching nutritional science. Too often when a physician is asked about the value of diet or specific vitamin supplements, the response is a rather tepid, non-committal, "You can try vitamins, they won't hurt you, but we get all we need in our foods, and they are largely a waste of money."

Because of the obvious success of complementary forms of medicine (acupuncture, chiropractry, and orthomolecular), mainstream medicine has slowly and begrudgingly begun to accept them; yet, it continues to be relatively uninformed in these areas. This dichotomy between western or mainstream medicine on the one hand and complementary medicine on the other is very unfortunate and a detriment to the nation's health. In a prefatory note to his book, *Alternative Medicine, A Definitive Guide*, editor Burton Goldberg writes, "Let me conclude by saying that I'm not against mainstream, conventional medicine. The Chinese have a saying about the wisdom of 'walking on both feet,' which means using the best of eastern and western procedures. That's what I want to see us do. There is no single approach that works for all people, or with all conditions." Goldberg admits conventional (western) medicine excels when it comes to surgery, emergency, and trauma, but contends Goldberg, complementary medicine is superior for so many other medical problems — "especially for chronic degenerative diseases like cancer, heart disease, rheumatoid arthritis, and for more common ailments such as asthma, gastrointestinal disorders, headaches, and sinusitis."

If not currently seeing a physician schooled in the prevention of disease rather than merely body repair, consider asking owners or managers of health food stores for the names of nutrition-minded physicians. Also, to obtain referrals to physicians trained in nutritional medicine, contact: American College of Advancement in Medicine/ P.O. Box 3427/ Laguna Hills, California 92654. ACAM provides an international directory of health practitioners trained in preventative and nutritional medicine. The ACAM directory also offers an extensive list of article and book titles on nutritional supplementation.

The book stores and health food stores will also feature an excellent library of books on vitamins, minerals, and herbs. With the current state of affairs, we have to be willing to do a good deal of reading and educate ourselves in preventative medicine; we have to take on some of the responsibility for our own health.

It does seem foolish, however, to launch a program of vitamin supplements without, at the same time, improving the diet itself. In addition to emphasizing the proper sequencing of protein and carbohydrate intake to guarantee high quantities of tryptophan (see Appendix B for the amount of tryptophan in the various foods) and adopting a supplement program like the one provided above, Adelle Davis suggests as an anti-stress formula fortified milk, fresh and/or desiccated liver, cooked green leafy vegetables, and wheat germ as a cereal or added to food. For further ideas on diet and nutrition, see Davis' *Let's Eat Right to Keep Fit* and her other best-seller of over twenty-five years, *Let's Get Well*. But also refer to *Nutrition Almanac* and *Prescription for Nutritional Healing* mentioned earlier in this chapter and to the numerous books on diet and nutrition listed under References.

6 Nutrition and the Psychotropic Drugs

"The physician heals,
Nature makes well."

— Aristotle

Doctors and manic-depressives alike must develop openness, flexibility, and patience in treating this disease. Psychiatrists, charged with the responsibility of diagnosing emotionally ill patients, assessing the plethora of new medicines (those that require a prescription and those that do not), and prescribing proper dosages of these medicines certainly face a challenge. Broadly speaking, the psychiatrist will choose from three categories of drugs in treating manic depression: the anti-manic agents, the antidepressants, and the mood stabilizers.

If the condition is acute mania, the psychiatrist will likely turn to a group of drugs known as neuroleptics most commonly used for schizophrenia. In an effort to decrease the excitement, slow down the racing thoughts, and stop hallucinations (hearing voices, etc.), the doctor can choose from any number of anti-manic agents: Haloperidol

(Haldol), Thioridazine (Melleril), Chlorpromazine (Largactil, Thorazine), or Trifluroperazine (Stelazine).

If the bipolar individual reports in a depressed state, the psychiatrist's choices are even more staggering. There are: the selective serotonin re-uptake inhibitors; e.g., Fluoxetine (Prozac), Sertraline (Zoloft), Paroxetine (Paxil), and Fluvoxamine (Luvox); the tricyclic antidepressants: Amitriptyline (Elavil), Desipramine (Norpramin), and Imipramine (Tofranil); and another group of antidepressants: Buproprion (Welbutrin), Nefazodone (Serzone), Venlafaxine (Effexor), and Phenelzine (Nardil). This list of antidepressants is by no means definitive and new drugs to lift mood come on the market constantly. In addition, the doctor has to factor in the possibility of ECT (electroconvulsive therapy) for more difficult and urgent cases involving depression.

The third major category features the mood stabilizers. These drugs are used principally in two ways: in combination with an anti-manic agent or antidepressant when the mood is unstable or as an ongoing maintanence drug between episodes of the illness. Doctors currently rely on one of three options for maintaining stable mood: lithium, carbamazepine (brand name, Tegretol), and valproic acid (brand name, Depakene or Depakote). Lithium has occupied center stage among these mood stabilizers since the late 70's and it is still first choice as a maintenance drug by most psychiatrists, but Tegretol and Depakote are gaining momentum. Increasingly Depakote gets the nod as a leveler for those individuals who tend more toward the manic than the depressive pole.

Known as anti-convulsants, Tegretol and Depakote are among a group of drugs originally developed as anti-seizure medication for epileptics. The history of these anti-convulsant drugs typifies the fantastic growth in psychotropic medicine. Tegretol and Depakote approved in 1963 and 1964 respectively for epileptics and in the 90's for bipolars are classified as second generation anti-convulsants. The first generation includes the bromides (1857), phenobarbital (1912), phenytoin (1940), primodone (1952), and ethosuximide (1958). As I have said, there is much enthusiasm right now over the increased use of the second generation of these drugs, Tegretol and Depakote; but we are already into the third generation: Vigabatrin (1992), Lamictal (1993), Neurontin and Felbatol (1995), and Gabatril (1996). As the explosion of this one type of psychotropic drug indicates, today's psychiatrists could occupy 90% of their time listening to pharmaceutical salesmen pitch their latest drugs.

But it isn't just the vast array of prescription drugs today's psychiatrists need to understand. They must also know what to tell their patients about the myriad of non-prescriptive agents increasingly in the news. Presently, it is St. John's Wort, but last year it was melotonin, for some time it has been tryptophan or 5-HTP, and there are many more. As I have said above, too often traditional or western medicine is slow to accept complementary forms of medicine. In many instances, these western doctors need to do their homework, understand the place of these naturally-occurring agents in the over-all scheme of pharmocology for emotional disease, and openly discuss these findings with their patients. Since nutrition and vitamin therapy — the neutraceuticals — are non-toxic, the psychiatrists should consider these natural medicines in combination with the harsher drugs. With some bipolar individuals, a significant amount of their medicine will be a prescription drug, but that is not always the case. And, as we will see in a later segment of this chapter, nutrition can play a significant role even in those instances when strong psychotropic drugs are required.

The Neutraceuticals

In order to understand the potential of St. John's Wort ("hypericum perforatum") for those with emotional disease, it is necessary to flip back to the "clinical construct" for depicting the evolution of the bipolar-unipolar distinction for manic-depressive illness early in chapter 3 and to refer as well to the "Fieve-Dunner Manic-Depressive Mood Scale" at the end of that chapter. St. John's Wort has only tangential efficacy for the manic-depressive as it can help lift the mood only for those with dysthymia or mild to moderate depression. So, if we look at the clinical construct, the herb might only apply to individuals with emotional disease on the far left wing of the diagram marked "unipolar;" moreover, the herb would be appropriate only for individuals coming part way down that line — just for those with mild to moderate unipolar depression. Or, if we look at the Fieve-Dunner Mood

Scale, St. John's could possibly be useful for those who demonstrate "noticeable lack of energy, chronic lack of optimism and pleasure, some sleep and appetite disturbance, etc." as observed in the 30 — 40 range on the depressive end of the scale.

At the present state in its research, there is no evidence that this agent — used as the sole medication -would be at all useful at the serious or severe ranges of the scale for either mania or depression. Nor does St. John's Wort have any real potential as a mood stabilizer or maintenance supplement for those subject to serious or severe mania or depression — in the same sense that lithium, Tegretol, or Depakote have that capacity (Bloomfield 1996). In the gallery of medicines useful for manic depression, these last three are major stars: St. John's Wort is just a bit player. And yet, this herb can be of great value and should be encouraged for those 12 to 15 million Americans who suffer from mild to moderate depression.

Individuals who have no history of mania and no record of severe or even serious depression are frequently referred to as reactive (situational) or neurotic depressives; and, when these individuals experience their mild to moderate lows these moods do sometimes involve the body chemistry: there are hormonal and neurotransmitter changes in the neuroendocrine system (Passwater 1977). But such involvement with the body chemistry is only marginal. These depressives are not significantly endogenic. For people who periodically suffer from this milder form of depression, an agent like St. John's Wort combined with psychotherapy and a diet featuring foods high in tryptophan and the supplements recommended in the "nutrient" chart in chapter 5 (5-HTP, B-complex, etc.) could be sufficient. But too often psychiatrists overmedicate and prescribe one of the high-powered SSRI's (selective serotonin reuptake inhibitors) like Prozac or Zoloft.

Dentists don't pull the tooth when they observe a minor cavity. We need to encourage psychiatrists to forego the heavy artillery when there are effective alternatives at much less cost. These herbs, amino acids, and megavitamins are more reasonably priced than the prescription drugs. But they are safer as well. Side effects with St. John's Wort, the amino acid 5-HTP, and the other nutrients indicated for depression are virtually non-existent. Prozac, on the other hand, has these side-effects: insomnia (trouble falling asleep or frequent waking during the night); nausea, diarrhea, or stomach cramps; headache; and nervousness. Prozac's less common side effects are drowsiness, serious weight loss, difficulty having an orgasm; hypomania (opposite of depression: patients become hyperactive, overly optimistic, and extremely talkative).

While all three mood stabilizers are certainly preferable to the symptoms of the disease, like Prozac and many psychotropic drugs they have important side effects. In rare cases, Tegretol can result in a condition called aplastic anemia in which the blood count can fall too low. Tegretol can also rarely interfere with liver, kidney, or thyroid function and blood tests must be taken every six months to a year. This drug can also cause a variety of skin reactions that require stopping the drug immediately. Initially, psychiatrists were prescribing Tegretol in combination with lithium — increasingly they are finding Tegretol to be effective on its own.

Depakote is an effective deterrant; however, it too has its share of side effects: nausea, vomiting, indigestion, and drowsiness sometimes occur. Generally, these toxicities are more prevalent when first on the drugs. It is very important in the case of Depakote to consistently monitor the liver and thyroid. While Tegretol can be combined with lithium therapy, these two drugs need to be cleansed from the system and Depakote taken alone.

In addition to effectively treating the mild to moderate forms of depression, St. John's Wort can be taken for more severe manic depression as a secondary medicine to one of the mood stabilizers like lithium or Tegretol. Like tryptophan and B-complex, St. John's Wort could reduce the need for the more toxic drugs and, thereby, diminish unwelcome side effects and improve compliance. Typically, these neutraceuticals work synergistically with the drugs; they will not cause adverse reactions with the drugs or undermine their benefits . Remember, St. John's Wort is a naturally occurring herb, tryptophan and 5-HTP simply amino acids (proteins), and B-complex, merely vitamins. These substances are not powerful drugs that would require the careful supervision of a professional psychiatrist. These are natural products available to us without prescription in health food stores, and often, in drug stores and supermarkets. My personal bias, however, is to restrict my consumption of neutraceuticals to reputable health food stores: some of these natural medicines absorb in the body better than others, and it is important we identify products of the highest quality whose actual potencies equate with that reported on the bottle.

While these neutraceuticals do not pose a serious threat to us, it is necessary we exercise a little common sense in their consumption. Aspirin is also, appropriately, available to us without prescription, but it can upset our stomachs and do far more if we do not use good judgment in taking it. Nutritional products are not any different. So, if St. John's Wort seems a sensible product to try, we must — at the very minimum — read the label on the bottle. There, we will find if we are presently taking monoamine oxidase inhibitors (MAOI's) we should not take the herb; or, if we are presently taking some other antidepressant we should consult with our doctor before starting this medicine. We are cautioned against taking St. John's Wort with other anti-depressants because the early research indicates the active ingredient in this herb is, at least in part, a serotonin reuptake inhibitor (Bloomfield 1996). Since many of the antidepressants also work because they too are SRI's, we are warned against what is called the "serotonin syndrome." It is possible the brain can get too much serotonin — the opposite of what we have with depression — and the following symptoms can result: lethargy, tremor, muscle jerks, agitation, sweating, and confusion." While this inordinate serotonin build-up is unlikely and can be easily reversed by merely cutting back on those agents contributing to serotonin levels, it does not hurt to be aware of this syndrome.

St. John's Wort can also interfere with the absorption of iron. Other herbs like garlic, ginger, ginkgo, and feverfew can increase the activity of prescription blood thinners like coumadin. Still other herbs, kava for instance, can increase the sedation of valium-type drugs. So while neutraceuticals generally complement and enhance the effectiveness of drugs, there are these and other exceptions. This is the reason we must always make our doctors aware of what we are ingesting in our bodies.

Nutrition and the Prescription Drugs

Nutrition can function importantly to reduce the degree of toxicity of any of the psychotropic drugs, but because of lithium's central role in treating bipolar disease I have chosen to focus on the benefits of nutrition for this effective mood stabilizer.

In his book, *The Essential Guide to Psychiatric Drugs,* psychiatrist Jack M. Gorman, M.D. writes, "Lithium has proven to be one of the true miracle drugs in psychiatry. About 80% of bipolar patients respond and remain symptom free. Those patients will certainly agree that the discoverer of lithium, Australian physician John Cade, and the man who proved that lithium works in bipolar patients, Scandanavian psychiatrist Mogens Schou, deserve a Nobel Prize. Lithium is safe and effective when administered under proper supervision. Any person with a serious bipolar disorder deserves a trial of lithium and should, in no way, fear this drug."

As we indicated earlier in this chapter, science has now developed the anti-convulsant drugs, Tegretol and Depakote, for the 20% for whom lithium has not proven effective, along with a number of other drugs proven effective for those with bipolar disorder. When lithium proves ineffective or particularly noxious to a patient, psychiatrists will now try one of these anti-convulsant drugs or lithium in combination with one of these two drugs or in combination with another drug(s) specific to either mania or depression. In this way, many of the 20% not treatable with lithium alone can now be significantly helped.

While lithium itself can help up to 80% as Dr. Gorman states, an insightful book by Monica Ramirez Basco, Ph.D. and A. John Rush, M.D., *Cognitive-Behavioral Therapy for Bipolar Disorder* claims a 46% noncompliance rate in taking the drug as prescribed. Although lithium — like many drugs — is considered dangerous for women during pregnancy, it is generally considered a very safe drug. I would just add parenthetically here, however, that anyone taking lithium would be well advised to purchase Mogens Schou's little book, *Lithium Treatment of Manic-Depressive Illness* where Dr. Schou thoroughly considers not only the efficacy of this drug but also its risk factors.

Some manic-depressives refuse to take lithium, however, not because of any potential danger but merely because it is a drug and they have difficulty accepting their illness. Other patients will not take lithium because of a few annoying side effects, but most of these such as nausea, hand tremor, dizziness, and metallic taste in the mouth disappear a few weeks after the treatment is under way — and many never experience these side-effects. Impaired co-ordination when driving, problems with adequate thyroid function, and weight gain can also accompany lithium consumption, but these too can normally be overcome. Because lithium has proven so successul in moderating highs and lows for such an overwhelming majority of manic-depressives every effort should be made to adjust to the side effects of this drug. As we have said, most of the side effects never appear or disappear after the first month or two. Some of the unwanted effects persist because patients do not drink sufficient quantities of water or take enough salt as they are instructed by their physician.

Still, we know from the Basco and Rush study — and from other studies as well — that problems of compliance with lithium do persist. Perhaps the most common complaint with this drug is that it dulls the mind and senses. Dr. Mogen Schou's study of a select group of manic-depressives with a profession demanding creative work claimed 25% had to give up lithium because of its tendency to inhibit intellectual and artistic creativity (Schou 1993).

Lithium's potential to stifle creativity suggests the importance of a close relationship between psychiatrist and patient and the need to test the lithium level in the blood frequently. Serum lithium level is determined by a measurement known as a mmol (millimole) per liter. One millimole is 7 mg of lithium ion. Most patients do well on a serum lithium level of 0.5 — 0.8 mmol/l. If they maintain this level of lithium in the blood, it prevents the symptoms of mania and depression with minimal side effects. A very few individuals can go as low as 0.3 mmol/l and still remain in an effective therapeutic range and, likewise, a miniscule number of other patients can be protected effectively against mania and depressive relapses only if their serum lithium level remains in the high range of 0.8 to 1.0 mmol/l. These higher lithium levels can be dangerous and can even induce poisoning (Schou 1993).

If the effective therapeutic range is 0.5–0.8mmol/l and noxious side effects are proportional to the lithium level, it follows that a bipolar patient would have less toxic side effects if the measure of serum lithium is kept in a low range. Some of the complaints bipolars have, then, regarding lithium's tendency to dull the mind and senses and to stifle creativity could possibly be overcome by the psychiatrist monitoring the lithium level more carefully — making sure the patient maintains the lowest level possible and yet stays within an effective therapeutic range.

How Lithium Works

The evidence suggests lithium impacts the HPA axis and neurotransmitter system, serotonin, so pivotal in controlling the corticotropin-releasing factor and determining an individual's response to stress. In addition to enhancing available serotonin, lithium appears to influence sodium and potassium reactions within nerve cells and to function importantly in the neuron's second messenger system.

Although the research on serotonin and other neurotransmitters is still at a relatively early stage, there is plenty science already understands. We have known for close to a quarter of a century, for example, that without serotonin, dopamine, and norepinephine and the hundreds of other known neurotransmitters, the brain could not process information or send out instructions to the rest of the body. This is because neurons, or nerve cells, do not actually contact one another; they are separated by gaps known as synapses. When the electrical impulses that move information through the nervous system reach the end of a neuron, they have nowhere to go. The circuit is broken.

That is, it would be, if not for the neurotransmitters. These molecules are stored in tiny sacs known as vesicles, located at the nerve endings. When an electrical signal reaches the vesicles, they release their load. The neurotransmitter molecules navigate across the synapse and lock into receptors on the neighboring nerve cell — an action roughly equivalent to turning on a light switch. The second nerve cell wakes up and sends off a jolt of electricity to pass the message along. Their job completed, the neurotransmitter molecules detach and are ferried back to be reabsorbed or destroyed.

The neurotransmitter story is, in reality, somewhat more complex than this as different neurons specialize in releasing different neurotransmitters; for example, some carry messages that concern patterns of light and sound and some carry messages of action, telling muscles when to release or contract.

But a small subset of these brain chemicals, especially serotonin, evidently serves an entirely different purpose. As Steven Hyman, director of the National Institute of Mental Health, describes it, "These neurotransmitters modulate raw information and give it an emotional tone." Northwestern University psychiatrist James Stockard puts it more poetically, "A person's mood is like a symphony, and serotonin is like the conductor's baton." Other neurotransmitters help us know our stomachs are full; serotonin tells us whether we feel satisfied.

Serotonin is so pervasive throughout the nervous system it is no wonder it plays such an important role. The nerve cells that specialize in serotonin production originate in the raphe nuclei, in a region right atop the spine that NIMH's Hyman calls the "deep basement of the brain." From there, these neurons extend vinelike projections called axons up through the brain and down into the spinal column. The axons form a sort of neurological interstate-highway network, over which serotonin supplies are sent to all parts of the nervous system. Other neurotransmitters are restricted to certain regions of the brain or body; serotonin is just about everywhere (Michael D. Lemonick 1997).

As we have said, conclusive evidence affirms lithium's capacity to improve serotonin's effectiveness. We learned in chapter 4 that lithium increases and stabilizes serotonin (Mandell and Knapp, 1979). We also know chronic lithium treatment has been associated with a marked augmentation of the 5-HTP-induced secretion of cortisol (Meltzer et al, 1984), a finding consistent with the previous reports that lithium facilitates serotonergic activity in animals (Goodwin 1990). And, we learn in a study by Slater and colleagues, 1976, that lithium has been reported to augment the fenfluramine-induced release of PRL, thus "adding to the consensus that lithium potentiates functional serotonin activity in a variety of systems."

We also discovered in our study of nutrition in chapter 5 that a combination of the B-complex vitamins and foods high in tryptophan will increase serotonin levels. Working in Surrey, England in the 1970's Drs. Arthur Prange, Alec Coppen, and Peter Whybrow "found that drugs which block the activity of serotonin neurons in the brain made mania worse — much worse. However, supplementing the diet with tryptophan, the amino acid from which the neurons manufacture serotonin, improved the treatment response in both mania and depression. Subsequently, other scientists discovered that reducing tryptophan in the diet can exaggerate depression, including seasonal depression, and that those suffering mania and depression have less of the breakdown products of serotonin in the cerebrospinal fluid of the brain — a finding that persists even into recovery and may be an indication of genetic vulnerability" (Whybrow 1997).

If the lithium and nutrition both accomplish the same goal of im-

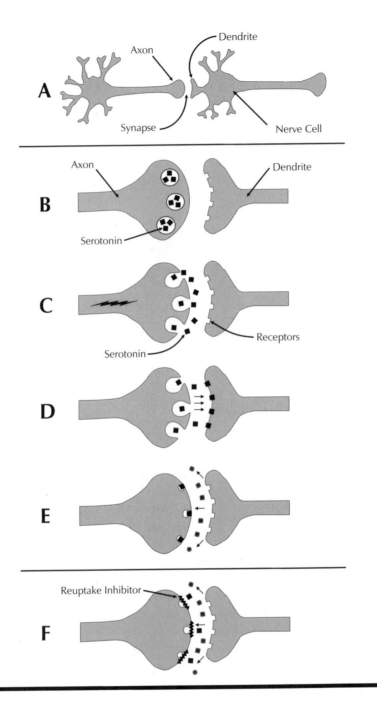

Figure 6-1. Neurotransmitters and the Selective Serotonin Reuptake Inhibitors

(Though not technically an SSRI, lithium strengthens serotonin action — see "F" facing page.)

The Great Divide

A. Nerve cells carry information in the form of electrical impulses. But to communicate with one another, the cells must get signals across the gaps, called synapses, that separate them. Neurotransmitters like serotonin are the messengers that bridge the gaps.

The Normal Cycle

B. Serotonin is stored in tiny sacs at the ends of the nerve cells.

C. Triggered by an electrical signal, these sacs merge with the nerve ending's outer membrane, releasing the neurotransmitter into the synapse.

D. Serotonin molecules diffuse across the gap and bind to specialized proteins, called receptors, on the surface of the second nerve cell.

E. When the serotonin's job is done, the receptors release the molecules, which are either broken down or reabsorbed by the first nerve cell and stored for later use.

The Reuptake Inhibitors

F. The Reuptake Inhibitors block the reabsorption of serotonin, thereby increasing its availability in the gap. While lithium, like the SSRIs, has the capacity to strengthen serotonin's presence in the synapse, its functions appear multiple and complex. See Figure 6-6.

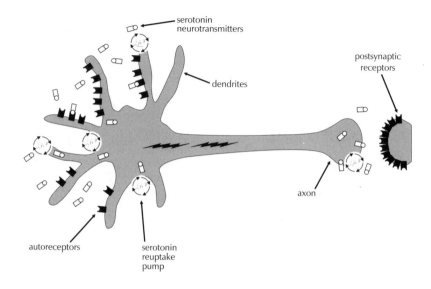

serotonin
neurotransmitters

postsynaptic
receptors

dendrites

autoreceptors

serotonin
reuptake
pump

axon

Early in this chapter we pointed out that lithium gives way to the SSRIs (selective serotonin reuptake inhibitors) and other "heavier" forms of antidepressant medication when a bipolar individual becomes severely depressed. In this figure we observe a serotonin neuron in a depressed patient. Note the serotonin neurotransmitters are relatively depleted. At the same time, the number of serotonin receptors is up-regulated, or elevated, including both the autoreceptors in the dendrite area of the cell and on the membrane of the neighboring neuron across the synapse.

Figure 6-2. A Serotonin Neuron in a Depressed Patient

proving the action of serotonin in the brain, it would seem logical that manic-depressives who take all or some of the neutraceuticals supplying serotonin would have a better chance of achieving an effective serum lithium level on the low end of the therapeutic range. And yet, it is of vital importance for most manic-depressives that we perceive the nutrition as supplemental to the drug and not a substitute for it. It would be wrong to assume that because we are supplying serotonin nutritionally that we can be casual and less exacting in monitoring our

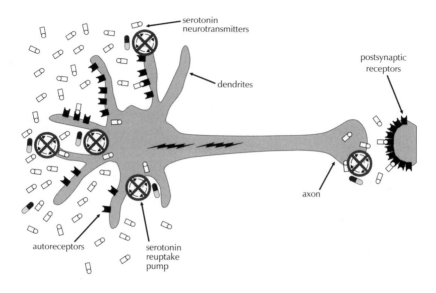

serotonin neurotransmitters

postsynaptic receptors

dendrites

axon

autoreceptors

serotonin reuptake pump

Note when an SSRI is applied, it begins immediately to block the serotonin reuptake pump (see the circled Xs at the axon and again at several points in the dendrites). Initially, however, this only causes an increase in the serotonin neurotransmitters in the dendrite area; there is no initial improvement at the axon terminals.

Figure 6-3. The Administration of the SSRIs

lithium intake. To take just a small amount of lithium in a random manner will not work: the drug must be kept in the effective therapeutic range (again, for most of us, 0.5 to 0.8 mmol/l) or we might just as well not be taking any lithium at all. So again, the importance of maintaining close contact with the health care provider: medications and symptoms must be monitored carefully at all times.

While St. John's, tryptophan, and the B-complex vitamins mirror lithium's capacity to increase serotonin and shore up the limbic

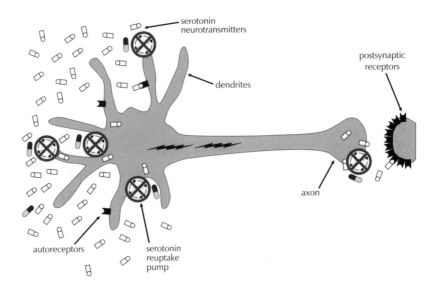

serotonin
neurotransmitters

postsynaptic
receptors

dendrites

autoreceptors

serotonin
reuptake
pump

axon

The consequence of serotonin increasing in the somatodendritic area of the serotonin neuron as depicted in Figure 6-3 is for the somatodendritic serotonin 1A autoreceptors to downregulate.

Figure 6-4. Mechanism of Action of SSRIs

centers of the brain, the lithium is thought to perform other actions the nutrition might not accomplish. Like the anti-convulsants, lithium decreases the excitability of the neuron, very likely altering the dynamics of the ions moving back and forth through the membrane wall. Lithium is also thought to modify the signaling of the second messenger systems within the neuron itself, disturbing the energy cycles that sustain the information transfer from the receptor to the nucleus.

It helps to think of the "first messenger system" as the signalling accomplished by the neurotransmitters moving across the synaptic gap between neurons; the "second messenger system," then, would be

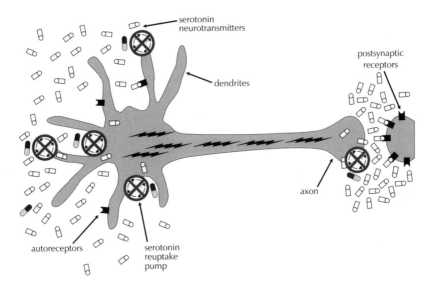

Once the somatodendritic autoreceptors downregulate as depicted in Figure 6-4, there is no longer inhibition of impulse flow in the serotonin neuron. Thus, neuronal impulse flow is turned on. The consequence of this is for serotonin to be released in the axon terminal. However, this increase is delayed compared to the increase in serotonin in the somatodendritic areas of the serotonin neuron depicted in Figure 6-3. This delay is the result of the time it takes for somatodendritic serotonin to downregulate the serotonin 1A receptors, and turn on neuronal impulse flow in the serotonin neuron. This delay may account for why antidepressants do not relieve depression immediately. It is also the reason why the mechanism of action of antidepressants may be linked to increasing neuronal impulse flow in serotonin neurons with serotonin levels increasing in axon terminals before an SSRI can exert its antidepressant effects (Stahl 1996).

Figure 6-5. Mechanism of Action of SSRIs

the movement of messenger molecules within the neuron itself that trigger a series of events resulting in the transfer of information into the nucleus and genetic library. Getting to the library is significant because this loci of the cell holds the blueprints required to produce the protein machinery — the receptors, enzymes, and transport systems

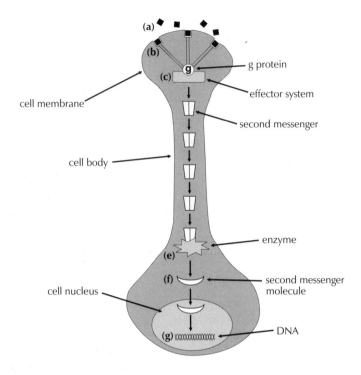

This figure shows the progress of a second messenger from the cell membrane to the cell nucleus. The first messenger **(a)** binds with the receptor **(b)**. The bound neurotransmitter causes an effector system **(c)** to create a second messenger. As the second messenger cascades down through the neuron to the cell's nucleus and the DNA, its chemical makeup will be altered by contact with enzymes **(e)**. The lithium is thought to impact the second messenger at stage **(b)** with the g protein and/or stage **(e)** with the enzymes.

The molecules **(f)** formed with the enzyme provide a special set of instructions for the cell's DNA **(g)**. Once the message with these special instructions has reached the DNA site, virtually any biochemical change conceivable is possible, since the DNA is the command center of the cell and has all the know-how and power to change any and all biochemical events of which the cell is capable.

One change typically ordered when second messenger molecules reach the DNA is the directive to slow down the synthesis of neurotransmitter receptors: this slowed down process is called "down regulation." When the inverse is true and the creation of receptors is increased, the process is known as "up regulation." The serotonin is thought to more effectively contact the receptors when they are in the "down regulation" position.

Figure 6-6. Lithium and Second Messenger Systems

— needed to maintain a healthy neuron and a flexible response to incoming information (Whybrow 1997).

The handoff of first messenger to second messenger is accomplished by means of a molecular cascade: neurotransmitter to neurotransmitter receptor (see Fig. 6-6); neurotransmitter receptor to "g protein;" binary complex of two proteins to an enzyme; and enzyme to second-messenger molecule.

As if this were not complex enough, the cascade put into motion by the first messenger and continued by the second messenger in fact does not stop here. The exact molecular events of this continuing cascade are the subject of intense current investigation and are just beginning to be unraveled. The cascade continues as second messengers change various cellular activities. For example, the second messenger can activate enzymes that are capable of altering virtually any function within the cell. One of the most important functions triggered by enzymes activated by second messengers is to change the membrane's permeability to ions such as calcium. Altering fluxes of ions in the neuron is one of the key ways to modify the excitability of the neuron that the second messenger is trying to influence.

Alternatively, in some neurons, second messengers can activate yet another enzyme to phosphorylate proteins and enzymes inside the cell. This process can alter the synthesis of various molecules in the cell that the second messenger wishes to regulate in order to modify the functioning of that neuron. Eventually, the message is passed along via messenger after messenger until the information reaches the cell nucleus and the DNA (genes) that is there. Once the message has been received at this site, virtually any biochemical change conceivable is possible, since the DNA is the command center of the cell and has all the know-how and power to change any and all biochemical events of which the cell is capable (Stahl 1996).

Because we know that for many bipolars enhancing serotonin levels can appreciably diminish symptoms, increasing selective neutraceutical intake might allow a lower lithium level; and yet, with the other properties that allow lithium to influence the second messenger system as well as the first we must vigilantly survey the lithium level and insure it is in an effective therapeutic range. The nutrition might very well allow a lower and still effective therapeutic range, but that might just as well not be the case, depending on which of the many and varied actions of lithium are particularly operative in maintaining the stability of the brain chemistry of any one individual. We must remember our objective in taking the nutrition is not to supplant the lithium entirely, but rather to attain a lower effective serum lithium level where we will experience less toxicity.

Nutrition's Other Benefits

In addition to nutritionally supplied serotonin potentially helping bipolars achieve an effective therapeutic range on the low end of the scale, nutrition therapy can help minimize side-effects in other ways. The individual who eats well balanced, nutritionally fortified meals and follows a vitamin/mineral formula such as the one provided in chapter 5 will construct healthy cells capable of detoxifying these psychotropic drugs. Vitamin C is especially helpful in combatting drugs, and manic-depressives would do well to take 3 to 6,000 mgs (6 grams) of this vitamin a day. A major function of vitamin C is its "non-specific role as a detoxifying agent;" (Nut. Rev. 1957) and for nearly 30 years it has been known to prevent the toxicity, allergic reactions, and anaphylactic shock caused by drugs. This vitamin appears to react with any foreign substance reaching the blood (Nut. Rev. 1946); and, if generously supplied, it nullifies the toxicity of fluorine, saccharine and other artificial sweetners, lead, benzene, carbon tetrachloride, and excessive vitamins A and D, as well as drugs. Yet all of these substances "destroy" vitamin C, causing it to be used up and excreted in the urine and, by the same token, tremendously increasing the need for it. The more toxic the drug, the larger the amount of the vitamin required. Rats given highly toxic cancer-producing drugs excrete 50 to 75 times more vitamin C than normally (A.H. Conney 1959).

The amount of vitamin C in human blood falls drastically when drugs are taken, particularly that of people showing drug reactions, sometimes even when 800 milligrams of the vitamin are given daily with a single dose of a drug. Such drugs as barbiturates, adrenaline, stilbestrol, estrogen, sulfonamides, ammonium chloride, aspirin, the antihistimines, thiouracil, thyroid, and atropine cause a continuous destruction and high urinary loss of the vitamin as long as the drug is taken and sometimes for six weeks after it has been discontinued (Davis 1989).

In *Nutrition Almanac* (1996), Kirschmann and Kirschmann provide additional evidence of Vitamin C's capacity to detoxify drugs when they claim large doses of the vitamin (from 25 to 85 grams daily for 4 days, then reduced to 10 grams) have been successfully used to help cure addictive drugs as stubborn as heroin and methadone. In *Supernutrition* (1976), Richard Passwater reports, "Dr. Herbert Sprince and his associates at the Veterans Administration Hospital in Coatesville, Pennsylvania used a spectrofluorometer to determine that vitamin C protects against acetaldehyde poisoning — acetaldehyde forms in the blood of alcoholics and heavy smokers and is a powerful initiator of dangerous free-radicals as well as being a cross-linking compound. A combination of certain sulfur amino acids and vitamin C gave 100 per cent protection against a standard lethal dose of acetaldehyde in laboratory rats. Dr. Fred R. Klenner has used vitamin C in high doses for years to detoxify many poisons, including snake venom, successfully.

In *Prescription for Nutritional Healing*, Balch and Balch list the amino acid, L-Glutathione, for its unique capacity to detoxify drugs and reduce their harmful effects. They suggest following the directions on the label for L-Glutathione and also for GABA (gamma-amino butyric acid). 500mgs three times daily of Vitamin B-5 (pantothenic acid) and B-3 (niacinamide) are also suggested to combat the ill effects of drugs.

So, while we clearly need scientifically sound studies that will demonstrate the degree to which nutrition will specifically detoxify lithium itself and other psychotropic drugs, the evidence we present above strongly indicates a positive result for that research. This is vitally important to bipolar patients because far too often a side effect such as a dulled mind and impaired creativity causes non-compliance with the drug. The result can be a costly attack of mania or even a deep depression ending in suicide.

Nature's Special Gift

As we have said earlier in this chapter, lithium shares the role of mood stabilizer with Tegretol and Depakote. Still, lithium continues to be the drug of choice — either alone or in combination — to maintain a level affect for the greatest share of bipolars. Now in its third decade as a major player in the United States for mood disorder, the drug merits on-going study and evaluation.

My mother's attack of mania late in life illustrates lithium's remarkable restorative powers for someone with this illness. Mother endured numerous attacks of both depression and mania extending from her thirties right through her eighties. Her emotional state was quite volatile, susceptible to extreme mood swings, but in her mid-seventies she suffered a fall that caused her to become particularly vulnerable to an attack of mania. She slipped in the bathtub and severely injured her elbow. The injury was so painful and slow to heal her physician prescribed cortisone. The steroids coupled with her tendencies under stress soon resulted in a full blown high.

When manic, mother demonstrated the typical litany of symptoms including insomnia, hyperactivity, paranoia, poor judgment, garrulousness, and hostility. When she endured these states, the target of her anger was inevitably my father — ironically, the one she loved the most. On one occasion she became so manic she swung at dad and knocked his pipe out of his mouth sending it clear across the room. This kind of gesture was so foreign to her character the family realized once again she would require hospitalization — in the past it had been depression, this time clearly for mania.

It broke our hearts, but the family made the arrangements to admit my seventy-six-year-old mother. She was taken to a small local psychiatric hospital. It was now 1979, however, and a dramatic change had occurred in the treatment of this disease. Thanks largely to the efforts of Ronald Fieve, M.D. and Mogens Schou, M.D. a new drug, lithium, was finally the prevalent drug for manic-depressives in the United States. The drug had been readily available to those in the UK and across western Europe in the late fifties and throughout the sixties, but Fieve, Schou and others had a protracted struggle bringing it to the states.

The doctors at the small psychiatric clinic put mother on lithium immediately upon admittance and there was little if any change in her mood for the first 10 to 12 days on the drug. Then, the family watched in amazement the 13th, 14th, and 15th days as the lithium began to take hold. The change was truly dramatic as day-by-day one could actually see mother shed the various symptoms of the mania and regain emotional stability. She was well enough to return home after just three weeks in the clinic.

A History

Lithium's efficacy for manic depression is so significant its slow introduction to the United States resulted in much unnecessary suffering
for countless individuals. The word comes from the Greek lithos
meaning stone and is one of our natural elements appearing on chemistry's periodic table with the other salts, sodium and potassium. Ronald Fieve relates in his seminal work, *Moodswing*, that the discovery of
the therapeutic effect of lithium in treating mania occurred in 1949,
and as it seems with so many major medical findings came about quite
by accident. John F. Cade, an Australian psychiatrist, believed urea to
be the toxic substance inducing manic states, and he found it in patients' urine. To test this hypothesis Cade injected uric acid into guinea
pigs, so he used lithium, which was able to form the most soluble salt,
lithium urate. When he injected lithium urate (and later lithium carbonate) into guinea pigs, however, they became lethargic instead of excited. After Cade had administered lithium carbonate to ten manic
subjects with dramatically positive results, he reported his first findings. Lithium, he claimed, restored manic patients to normal mood
states, and on maintenance doses several of his more chronic and
hopeless patients became well enough to leave the hospital.

Lithium's significance becomes clear only when we place it
against the assorted methods man has used in treating mania over the
centuries. For several thousand years, — the most enlightened civilizations resorted to euthanasia, imprisonment, chains, and forceful re-
straints; the list of treatments took such forms as exotic potions, blood-
letting, and electric eels applied to the skull. Then came more modern
methods: insulin coma, lobotomy, electroconvulsive shock therapy,
psychoanalysis, and psychotherapy, and most recently the vast array
of newly synthesized tranquilizers and antidepressants. But not until
the advent of lithium did any form of treatment succeed for long in
bringing moodswing under control." Dr. Fieve concludes that "today
lithium controls and prevents recurrence of the chronic and debilitating moodwings typical of manic-depressives — and lithium is also
clearly effective in preventing recurrent depressions, even when manic
episodes are not present" (Fieve 1989).

Use Predates Cade

Well over 100 years before John Cade discovered lithium's efficacy for mania, it was used in the management of assorted medical problems such as gout, diabetes, and epilepsy. As early as 1845, lithium was used as a preventative in the treatment of both gravel and gout. In 1876 Garrod concluded uric acid deposition in brain tissue caused mania and depression, which were incorporated into the group of gouty diseases, and recommended the use of lithium — containing mixtures of alkaline salts. Karl Lange, a Danish neurologist, added another 'gouty' condition which he named "periodic depression" and treated with lithium.

Lithium was first entered into the list of pharmaceuticals available in the UK in 1864 and by 1910 there were 25 preparations available for a variety of medical conditions. In the USA lithium was marketed in the late 1940's as a substitute for ordinary table salt for patients requiring salt-free diets. Its liberal use resulted in many deaths from lithium poisoning. This led the Food and Drug Administration to bar its use for about 20 years before it was released again in 1970 for use in mania and in 1974 as a maintenance treatment.

Mania

The research tells us lithium is the medication of choice for mania except for highly active or disturbed patients who require certain antipsychotic drugs called neuroleptics that rapidly control the condition; these neuroleptics are often used in combination with lithium for these severe manic states. Quite often, the neuroleptics can be withdrawn within 2-3 weeks, by which time lithium's effects are well established. Lithium is less effective in mania patients with paranoid-destructive features than in those with grandiose-euphoric features (Murphy & Beigel 1974). Manic patients tolerate high doses of lithium due to increased influx into the intracellular space, but tolerance for the drug drops with improvement in association with increased plasma lithium levels. This necessitates frequent monitoring of lithium levels to prevent intoxication during recovery.

Acute Depression

Lithium has proven effective with depression as well as mania. Mendels, for instance, did a controlled placebo substitution study in 1976 and demonstrated definite antidepressant effects of lithium. Further studies have confirmed Mendels' findings: 10 out of 13 studies showed lithium to be superior to placebo, or as effective as tricyclic antidepressants (Fieve & Peselow 1983). In these studies lithium was effective in 43% of unipolar patients, 60% of bipolar II patients and 76% of bipolar I patients. It is important we note a study by Worrall and his colleagues (1979) indicated the clinical effects of lithium did not occur until the second or third week of treatment. Furthermore, the research suggests lithium tends to be more effective for those with bipolar than with non-bipolar disease. In the non-bipolar group of depressives, those with an endogenous symptom profile, family history of mania, cyclothymic personality (a mood disorder characterized by numerous manic and depressive periods with symptoms like those of manic and major depressive episodes but of lesser severity), and those whose depression seems triggered by effects of child birth tend to respond more favorably.

Lithium can, therefore, be strongly recommended for the treatment of bipolar depression rather than tricyclics which may provoke minor manic episodes and increase the risk for the development of rapid-cycling illness. There is evidence lithium alone is effective in depression that has failed to respond to tricyclic medication and in combination with other antidepressants in the management of resistant depression.

So, while lithium has a definite role with even the most resistant depressions, its unique set of properties make it most effective in reducing manic highs and in serving as a mood leveler and maintenance drug. In most cases, the enduring, stubborn depression (especially when suicidal tendencies are evident) are relieved by electroconvulsive therapy and/or the newest designer antidepressants, like Prozac and Zoloft. While lithium's action increases serotonin's efficacy, Prozac, Zoloft, and other SSRIs are even more precisely designed to enhance serotonin's role in fighting the most severe depression. But, like the lithium, both the Prozac and Zoloft can induce a number of unwanted side effects. Here again the tryptophan in certain foods (see Appendix A & B) combined with B-complex and the other relevant neutraceuticals can supply serotonin, reduce the need for the higher dosages of these drugs, and diminish the toxic effects. As we stated above in discussing nutrition and lithium, it is important the nutrition be a supplement to the drug and not a substitute for it. Behavior symptoms must be carefully balanced against the use of the nutrition and drugs and blood levels of the lithium, Prozac, Zoloft, or whatever particular drug prescribed assiduously monitored by the doctor.

Lithium as Preventative

Studies of the preventative potential of lithium have been impressive. Manic depression is a recurrent illness and the discovery of the preventative effects of lithium opened a new era in its management. In a number of controlled studies of varying degrees of disciplined scholarship, lithium was shown to substantially reduce the long term disease state of both unipolar and bipolar disorders. An early study by Baastrup and Schou in 1967 showed that, in a group of 88 patients with affective disorders who had received lithium for periods of up to 5 years, actual disease states of manic depression were reduced to 2 weeks a year from an average of 13 weeks a year before lithium. These results were confirmed in studies of similar design (Angst et al 1970, Hullin et al 1972).

A second phase of lithium preventative efficacy was the discontinuation trial. Patients who were maintained on lithium for years were randomly switched to receive placebo or to continue with lithium. Discontinuation of lithium therapy for a period of 5 months was associated with relapse of 54% of patients compared with no relapse in patients who continued on lithium (Baastrup et al 1970).

The next step was a test known as prospective trials. Coppen and his colleagues (1971) carried out the first placebo-controlled double-blind study of lithium over a period of 27 months. The results showed a very convincing advantage for the lithium-treated group. Patients who had received placebo and a variety of conventional treatment, including antidepressants, ECT or neuroleptics, spent 27% of their time as inpatients and a further 19% of their time with outpatient episodes. By contrast, patients treated with lithium spent only 5% of their time as inpatients and 7% of their time with an outpatient episode. The need for conventional treatment was also greatly reduced.

Two studies by Prien and colleagues (1973a,b) followed. The first was a placebo-controlled study for a period of 2 years; the second was a comparative study of placebo, lithium, and imipramine, a tricyclic antidepressant. In unipolar depressives both lithium and imipramine had a preventative effect, but in bipolar patients lithium was significantly better than imipramine.

Overall, lithium is more effective in the prevention of bipolar as opposed to unipolar illness. This appears to be related to bipolar patients sharing similar body chemistry as opposed to unipolar patients whose depression emanates from various causes making them more difficult to classify. This relates to the Sachar study cited in chapter 4 wherein over 50% of depressed patients were shown to have increased levels of cortisol. In referring to the study, we suggested the 50% figure would likely have been significantly higher if all those depressed patients included had been clearly identified as victims of endogenous disease. In other words, the evidence implies lithium clearly works for those with mania and for those with depression — but is particularly indicated for those whose emotional swings are endogenous; i.e., genetic and the result of body chemistry.

Whatever it is that goes awry in the biochemistry of manic-depressives, lithium seems to be nature's special gift to control it. Earlier (chapter 4) we made a study of the neuroendocrine system and the chemical changes that occur with an episode of manic depression. The potent antipsychotic tranquilizers and antidepressant compounds synthesized and marketed in the late 1950's relieve the symptoms of psychosis, anxiety, and melancholy associated with manic depression, but do not specifically get at the core of the illness. Dr. Fieve points out that lithium, by contrast with the tranquilizers and antidepressants, biochemically assaults and controls the illness itself — and is the first drug to do so.

Fine Tuning the Lithium Level

Earlier in the chapter we discussed the importance of maintaining an effective serum lithium level. The ultimate challenge in lithium use is maintaining a blood level within the therapeutic range, one that prevents manic and depressive symptoms, and a level that allows the patient to function effectively and feel well. If lithium therapy is to be successful in the long term, this three-part challenge must be met. We would be something less than candid if we were to imply this is an easy task.

My own quest to fine tune my lithium level is, in many ways, typical. As an English teacher I found if my lithium level was too high I was apt to become lethargic inhibiting my capacity to respond to the literature I was teaching or my speech became so slow and halting I put my students to sleep. At such times, I consulted with my psychiatrist and together we agreed to adjust the lithium level: instead of taking two 450 mg tablets every day, we decided to reduce that amount slightly on a temporary basis with the understanding that I decrease the interval between lab visits to be certain the level of lithium in the blood remained in the therapeutic range.

On the other hand, if the situation was reversed and my lithium level fell too low and it was an occasion when I was especially tired and/or under enormous stress, I ran the risk of unfairly reprimanding a student. Some days driving to work I knew I was dead tired, stressed to the limit with papers to grade and lessons to prepare, and my lithium at a precarious level. On such days my emotions might be such I could respond sensitively to the rhythm and tone of a Shakespearean sonnet, but, at the same time, I would be so brittle I was apt to receive a negative remark on my annual teaching evaluation for offending a student, parent, or administrator.

While it can be very challenging to maintain a suitable lithium level, it is imperative adjustments always be made in consultation with the psychiatrist. On one occasion I decided to go off lithium without discussing it with my psychiatrist and paid for it dearly. In 1986-87 I took a year's sabbatical with my wife and child to study and travel in England and decided to go on a lithium "holiday" since I surmised I would be under very little stress that year. I seemed fine until I accepted an assignment with Educational Testing Service to fly back to the states for 10 days to grade Advanced Placement Tests. The work with ETS was stressful, I was experiencing jet lag, and, after long, arduous days of grading, I slept poorly. By the end of the week, I was already in a manic state.

Although my wife and child were waiting for my return to England, I decided without ever discussing the matter to move our furniture from our home in Grand Rapids, Michigan to Princeton, New Jersey where I was working for ETS and rent an apartment for us there. I also decided I would leave the teaching profession after twenty years and find a new career in New Jersey. Part of this bizarre activity was grounded in sanity as it represented something of a mid-life crisis, a career teacher tightening up in the stretch drive wanting desperately to do something different with his life; and yet, to make such a decision without the knowledge and support of my family was entirely foreign to my character and clearly a symptom of manic behavior.

Surely, from such an experience we can infer the importance of close consultation with the psychiatrist regarding the use of lithium and maintaining a serum lithium level in the effective therapeutic range. We must remember that the poor judgement characteristic of my mania attack at Princeton influenced others as well as myself. Think of the trauma for my ten-year-old child to think she was leaving her neighborhood and friends as her father moved her home from Grand Rapids to Princeton and the added grief and stress for my wife who was not well at the time. And, all too often, the misguided financial endeavors or sexual promiscuity that accompany mania attacks result in far more tragedy than that experienced by my family. Moods, emotions, and the biochemistry of manic-depressives are so volatile and change can occur so subtly and suddenly we just cannot decide on our own to manipulate the amount of lithium.

While that lesson is clear, my manic escapade in Princeton highlights another point we make in chapter 4 concerning the role of stressful recent life events in manic-depressive attacks. I made my ill-advised decision to go off the lithium because I reasoned I would only be traveling and studying and not under the stress I normally experienced when teaching. While it worked out I was spared professional stress during most of 1986/87, the fates more than compensated with personal stress. Within weeks of our arrival in England, my wife was diagnosed with melanoma cancer (the worst of the skin cancers and a fatal disease), my mother was in the last few months of her life with heart disease, and my brother was in the throes of a bad bout with bipolar disorder. The Holmes-Rahe Social Adjustment Rating Scale is a test created in the late sixties to quantify the probability of enduring a health "breakdown" as a result of stressful events. A number from 11 to 100 is assigned to 53 different life events depending on the degree of stress and a total score of 300 or more over any one year is considered a high score and health threatening. My score for 1986/87 was 530, some 230 points in excess of what's considered the danger point.

As the three traumatic situations involving the health of close family members began to unfold in the fall and winter months of 1986/87, I should likely have known enough to reverse my decision regarding my need for lithium. Throughout that sabbatical year I had remained on the Brewer's Yeast (B-complex vitamins) my aunt had suggested back in my early twenties, but I had not yet learned of the other serotonin-producing neutraceuticals (St. John's Wort, trypto-phan, melatonin, etc.) Even at that, the B-complex kept me stable throughout that difficult year until the jet lag and the test grading proved too much.

As I say, I should have known enough to go back on the lithium. Too often, however, we are not particularly conscious of the pressures we are under or will be under at any one time. A second lesson, then, in my little Princeton saga is that bipolar individuals seek a level of well-being in taking lithium (or the maintenance drug proven most ef-fective for them). In this way, they will not be tempted to take lithium "holidays," — to go completely off the drug as I did. We can logically conclude that the vast array of neutraceuticals available today com-bined with stress reduction strategies will help the bipolar patient maintain a lower effective serum lithium level and, thereby, facilitate the desired comfort zone with the drug.

Neutraceuticals *and* Drugs

We can understand why psychiatrists tend to prescribe the more toxic psychotropic drugs. People typically resist seeing their doctor until their symptoms are quite extreme. To bring severe mania or a deep, persistent depression under control, the doctor turns to the more po-tent psychotropic drugs. There is most definitely a "Toxicity to Thera-peutic Ratio" with most drugs — meaning the best results are, unfor-tunately, accompanied by the highest toxicity. And, the simple truth is that some of us with bipolar disease will require the more selective drugs with the higher toxicities not just when we initially report — but very likely on an on-going basis if we expect to remain anywhere near symptom free. These potent psychotropic drugs,then, most definitely have their place and should be considered — despite their toxicities — a blessing. But what we have been able to show here is that the neutraceuticals have their place as well, and that through their more extensive use — sometimes in combination with the stronger drugs, sometimes alone, doctors can better minister to the total well-being of their patients.

7 Sleep Disturbance: A Core Symptom

"— the innocent sleep
Sleep that knits up the ravell'd sleave of care,
The death of each day's life, sore labour's bath,
Balm of hurt minds, great nature's second course,
Chief nourisher in life's feast."

— Macbeth

Psychiatrists specializing in the diagnosis and treatment of manic depression have commented on the tendency of manics to "need little sleep." Manics operate with high energy, creativity, and often accomplish incredible feats; a major change occurs in the body chemistry propelling these individuals into this frantic state. They are like the spendthrift, however, borrowing disproportionately against a finite bank account. In the end, many manic-depressives come full circle and suffer a low often more devastating in its crippling despair than was the exhilaration of the high. The manic stage, particularly at the onset, is pleasurable because of the mood of expansion and the satisfaction accompanying the increased activity and output. The manic does not feel sick and has no inclination to treat these moods until it is too late.

My mother's sleep pattern typifies the bipolar patient at the onset of an attack. When well, mother had a busy, purposeful, and fulfilling life. She taught fourth grade, performed the duties and requisites of a wife, looked after the various demands and needs of her four children, attended meetings of a local hospital guild and her Episcopal Church guild, attended functions of the city's ladies literary club, and subbed in the neighborhood bridge club. Mother was an active, productive person, and, in a reasonable and normal state of mind, knew she needed the summer break from her teaching to offset her hectic life during the academic year. In the summer of 1956, however, she felt the family needed some extra money and decided to open a summer playschool in our backyard. This venture was very successful from a professional and financial perspective; yet, by late September, mother had sustained a full blown depression.

Early Morning Waking

In the late spring and into the summer mother was supercharged with her new venture. She needed little sleep and was very energetic and creative in pulling together staff and materials for her summer school. By mid-September, her mood had changed dramatically. Whereas just weeks before she had seemingly required so little sleep, she now experienced acute anxiety over sleep. Shortly after returning to her full-time teaching duties in the fall, she began waking in the early morning hours and found she could not relax and go back to sleep. She became anxious and more and more obsessed with doubt, worry, and loss of confidence. Soon, she lost significant amounts of weight and became so tired and depressed she could not even enjoy her own family and friends — let alone work. By October 1, mother had been admitted to a local hospital for the mentally ill. She did not return home for nine months.

Research Links Insomnia to Depression

The majority of patients with major depressive illnesses demonstate sleep continuity disturbance usually observed as increased wakefulness or difficulty maintaining sleep. While younger depressive patients sometimes complain of difficulty falling asleep, middle-aged and older depressive patients (as observed in mother's attack of 1956) are more likely to report difficulty maintaining sleep, including the early morning waking.

The importance of sleep disturbance as a core symptom of mood change was recently highlighted by the National Institute of Mental Health study of sleep disturbances and psychiatric disorders (Ford and Kamerow 1989). The major finding in this study of 7954 respondents was that 40 .4% of those with insomnia and 46.5% of those with hypersomnia (tendency to sleep too much) had a psychiatric disorder, as compared to 16.4% of those with no sleep complaints. Ford and Kamerow also reported that the risk of developing a new major depressive episode was much higher in those patients who had insomnia both at an initial interview and again at a follow-up interview one year later as compared to those patients whose insomnia had disappeared by the time of the one-year follow-up interview. These data suggested the possibility that sleep disturbance might be critical in determining the cause of mania and depression, and that early recognition and treatment of sleep disturbance could prevent future psychiatric disorders.

Abnormality in REM Sleep

Brain activity during sleep can be measured by means of an electroencephalogram (EEG). Different stages of sleep are recognized by different EEG wave patterns. Drowsiness or stages 1 and 2 of sleep are marked by short irregular waves; as sleep deepens in stages 3 and 4 the waves become slower, larger, and more regular. These four stages of slow-wave sleep (NRem or Non-rapid eye movement sleep) are periodically interrupted by episodes of REM (rapid eye-movement sleep) when the EEG pattern is similar to that of an awake and alert person. Dreaming occurs during REM sleep. The two states of sleep,

NREM and REM, alternate in cycles of from 30 to 90 minutes, REM sleep constituting about a quarter of the total sleeping time.

Both the REM and NREM stages of sleep have proven to be of interest as a link to depression. Giles (1988), for example, has restricted most of his research to the REM stage and has shown that reduced stages of these sleep periods in an individual are associated with lifetime prevalence of depression. Giles also showed the risk for unipolar depression among relatives with reduced REM stages of sleep was almost three times greater than for relatives with non-reduced REM stage. And, as we observed in chapter 4, because of the action of specific peptide hormones linked to the hypothalamic-pituitary-adrenal axis, NREM or slow wave sleep is decreased in manic-depressives as well.

Improving Sleep

When a manic-depressive has reached the severe or extreme stages of the disease at either the mania or depressed poles as described by the Fieve-Dunner Manic-Depressive Mood Scale (see chapter 3), there is no alternative except to see a psychiatrist immediately. The doctor will then start the patient on lithium, one of the many antidepressants, electroconvulsive treatment, or some combination of these and/or other therapies to alleviate the extreme mood state and to correct the problems with sleep as well. But our interest here is with prevention; that is to say, with what manic-depressives can do while still in the moderate ranges of the disease to stabilize their own sleep patterns and, thereby, help prevent the more severe mood states. We are now more certain than ever that sleep patterns are disrupted because some stressor, sometimes very slight, has excited the endocrine system and its hormonal mix (steroid, thyroid, gonadal, and pineal).

Most of us become overwrought with weariness and extreme stress from time to time making it difficult to experience a good night's sleep. However, like the person beset with weight problems we tend to reach for a drug (the "silver bullet") rather than adopt an approach marked by discipline and common sense. The pharmaceutical companies make millions on sleeping pills and tranquilizers, but these drugs leave us hung over in the morning, generally undermine our health, and provide a temporary fix at best.

Sleep and Diet

In many instances the sleeping pills we ingest at bedtime are necessitated by the poor choices we make in diet during the day. For example, most of us are victimized by caffeine and very likely manic-depressives more than most because of their highly sensitive endocrine system. So it is necessary to avoid foods with caffeine in them like coffee, tea, most of the colas, and chocolate. Other substances and foods to avoid, particularly in the late afternoon and evening hours, are alcohol, sugar, tobacco, cheese, sauerkraut, bacon, ham, sausage, eggplant, potatoes, spinach, and tomatoes. These foods either contain sugar or tyramine. The foods containing tyramine promote norephinephine, a brain chemical stimulant; these foods help combat depression, but we need to be aware that consumed in the latter part of the day they can also disrupt sleep.

While our poor choices in food and drink help keep us susceptible to insomnia and the drug companies grossly rich, a little wisdom in our dietary habits could virtually ensure sleep. For example, foods high in the amino acid, tryptophan, promote sleep. To make certain we receive ample quantities of this protein, we need to consume plenty of turkey, bananas, figs, dates, yogurt, tuna, and whole grain crackers or nut butter (Balch 1990). A grapefruit half at bedtime also helps induce sleep. While prescription and over-the-counter sleeping pills provide only temporary relief and prove deleterious to the body, there are minerals and herbs occurring naturally that benefit sleep and nourish the body. If insomnia is a problem, take 1500 mgs of either calcium lactate or calcium chelate and 750 mgs of magnesium after meals and at bedtime. It is important calcium and magnesium supplements are taken together as these minerals work in tandem in the body. Also, take vitamin B-complex and extra amounts of vitamin B-5 and B-6 and inositol after meals. Valerian root (capsules or extract), catnip, EZcaps, hops, lady slipper, passionflower, and skullcap are all herbs proven effective to induce sleep. Another herb, St. John's Wort, and the natural hormone, melatonin — considered in the previous chapter — are proven benefits to sound sleep. These mega doses of calcium and magnesium, the B vitamins, and the various sleep-promoting herbs are all readily available in health food stores(see chapter 5).

Sleep and Exercise

I sustained a major attack of bipolar disease at eighteen and ultimately found relief at a progressive mental health clinic. During the early stages at this hospital when still very sick it was necessary I be detained in a basement lock-up segment of the institution because the paranoia often consistent with a bipolar attack induces the patient to resist help and even run away. However, once I had been at the institution for three or four weeks and had received a series of treatments, I was feeling considerably better and allowed to leave the lock-up and take a room upstairs. There was a dramatic difference between the two segments of the facility: the basement was cement block, gray and dingy, and with its locked corridors more akin to a jail than a hospital; the upper floors resembled a somewhat dated, but first class, hotel. There were private rooms with a bath, little kitchenettes proximate to the rooms for snacks, a lounge for TV watching, and a lovely dining room with all the amenities. Here, I could relax, convalesce, and regain some degree of balance and self-confidence before I was released to go home and confront the world once again.

During my stay in this upstairs portion of the clinic, my doctors sought to nurture my stressed central nervous system back to optimum health; and, exercise was a very significant part of my convalescence. The clinic even had a small gymnasium where I was encouraged to play basketball, but more than the workouts in the gym I benefitted from the walking regimen my doctors and nurses required me to take on a regular basis. The institution located on a major highway had an extensive circular driveway separating it from the road. If the weather was the least bit cooperative, I was expected to walk that driveway for an hour each afternoon.

My stay at the mental health clinic at eighteen dates back several decades, but I continue to value my doctor's insistence I tour the circular drive. Walking has become habitual in my daily routine and plays a principal role in my over-all strategy to prevent attacks of bipolar disease. As we observed in chapter 4, Dr. Hans Selye initially studied man's response to stress by examining animals' reactions to a variety of conditions — infection, cold, and fatigue. In Selye's development of G.A.S. (the general adaptation syndrome), he determined through countless laboratory tests that an animal's reaction to these kinds of conditions, whether they were physical or psychological, always tends to be the same. The blood pressure begins to rise, the heart starts to beat faster, and the pupils dilate. Stress will cause these identical physical responses in humans, but it will also make us moody, anxious, fearful, and depressed. What my doctor knew and I learned is that walking can be one of the most effective measures for combatting these stressors we encounter everyday. If we walk late into the evening hours, it can prove too stimulating; but, if we time a 30 minute to an hour walk late in the afternoon or early evening, it stimulates us initially but by bedtime proves very restful and beneficial to sleep.

We sometimes find it difficult to accept that an activity so natural to us as walking can be effective in relieving one of the most significant detriments to our health, but studies prove walking alleviates the psychological and physical effects of stress and, thereby, a major obstacle to sound sleep. Walking has been called a "eustress," or good stress, because it provides both the energy and tranquility to combat life's trials and frustrations, its distress.

Walking neutralizes stress as it enhances our energy level and, at the same time, reduces tension (Yanker and Burton 1993). The nature and circumstances of modern life will inevitably cause our palms to sweat and blood pressure to rise, but we cope much better when we allocate 10-15 minutes during lunch and/or 30-60 minutes in the evening for a walk. Tension is actually meant as an asset to man, an adaptive mechanism of the sympathetic nervous system that enables us to effectively manage our trials. When allowed to build, however, tension will only frustrate and disable. Too often, we then lose control and confront an associate or a supervisor in a manner we later regret. In its very essence bipolar disease involves our emotions and there are occasions when tension has the upper hand, but walking helps us diffuse most stressful situations, maintain a quiet serenity, and sleep soundly at night.

Walking is just one of the many modes of exercise helpful to sound sleep and improved health. I emphasize walking because it is an activity so accessible we are more inclined to do it on a daily basis — and because it is so inexpensive. But so many of the sports we love (golf, tennis, running, biking, etc.) should be encouraged as well. According to Dr. Edmund Bourne, author of *The Anxiety & Phobia Workbook*, exercise does the following:

- Increases feelings of well-being
- Reduces dependence on alcohol and drugs
- Reduces insomnia
- Improves concentration and memory
- Alleviates symptoms of depression
- Gives greater control over feelings of anxiety
- Increases self-esteem

A woman who has had episodes of depression for 15 years, and who now has her depression under control, says:

> I feel physically and emotionally better when I keep up with my exercise routine.

Another who has been well for 10 years says:

> I walk about two miles twice a week and bicycle for a mile once a week. It gets my mind off my problems and burns unused energy.

Dr. Wayne London, author of *Principles of Health*, recommends that we get three to five 30-to-45 minute sessions of aerobic exercise each week. If we are badly out of shape, however, it is a good idea to start with just a few minutes and gradually work up to the desired time. If we start too fast, the resulting aches and pains can discourage us from continuing. A warm bath after exercise can help reduce those aches and pains.

Therapeutic Baths

Water has been used for remedial purposes since time immemorial. Natives in various parts of the earth sought the healing effect of natural waters, mineral springs, sea water, rivers and springs. When medical science saw its birth, healing disease with water was recognized as one of the most important therapeutic modalities. Hippocrates, Celus, Galen and other ancient greats of medicine praised water for its many curative properties. In all major ancient civilizations, bathing was held in esteem not only for its remedial properties, but as an important health-building and disease-preventative measure.

In modern times, the therapeutic properties of water were popularized by Father Kneipp, Maria Schlenz, Priessnitz, and other European water-cure pioneers. There are hundreds of Spas and "Bads" in most European countries where therapeutic baths are used as a major healing measure, especially so-called Kneipp-baths. As Father Kneipp said, "Water contains great healing power" — and millions of yearly visitors to these "bads" can testify that water, indeed, does possess great therapeutic value (Airola 1974).

In addition to walking and other forms of exercise, my doctors at the progressive mental health clinic prescribed a bath everyday just before the evening meal. The hospital orderlies made sure I followed the assigned procedure. Thus, every afternoon at 4:30 or 5:00 P.M. I would draw a hot bath. It was a deep bath — clear to my chin — as hot as I could comfortably stand it; and, I was expected to remain in the tub for 45 minutes to an hour.

Most of us know how conducive a hot shower can be to a good night's sleep. One of the therapeutic baths — such as those I learned to take at the clinic — are many times more effective than a hot shower. In fact, when I begin to mount the symptoms of a mania attack (fitful sleep, general restlessness, mind jumping with ideas, etc.), I find a hot shower does little to relax me. But a series of the 45 minute to an hour therapeutic baths will begin immediately to ease my torqued-up nervous system and return it to a state of balance and equilibrium.

If we live with this disease long enough, we can sense the emergence of one of these manic highs early on. It might be just some minor life event, a loss of sleep, or some seemingly inconsequential incident that will activate the stress, energy, sexual, and rhythmic messenger systems and send their corresponding hormones (the steroid, thyroid, gonadal, and pineal) into orbit. I am personally very susceptible to these hormonal upsets, but find if I stay on my meds and megavitamins, follow a good walk with a therapeutic bath, and follow a diet high in tryptophan (see chapters 5 & 6 and Appendix B) I can regain control of these wayward chemicals.

Sleep and Meditation

There is a kind of paradox at the heart of contemporary life. At the same time that technology has brought unprecedented material comfort into our lives we have increased anxiety and unhappiness. We are learning the hard way that creature comforts have only marginally to do with personal fulfillment. The machines and gadgets of today's world have not only proven unfulfilling and disappointing, they are products of a technological era that place inordinate pressure on us. Allan Toffler's book, *Future Shock,* now over twenty years old calls our attention to the frantic pace of our contemporary world and its damaging effect on human life.

The information explosion is just one aspect of Toffler's thesis. We are asked to digest in a week what generations past were expected to assimilate over several years. We are inundated with facts, statistics, evidence on every side of a myriad of issues and products to the point of damaging overstimulation. While jet aircraft, extensive computer data banks, and hi tech production have greatly expanded the domain of man's influence, these developments have also proven very taxing to man's mind and senses. Toffler's term "future shock" refers to this inability of man to adjust to such an incredible amount of change in such a short time span. Toffler's insights imply that too much change too fast threatens the well being of man and impoverishes his emotional and mental health.

When an individual becomes victim to this relentless change, his body must respond to this pressure. The incessant pace requires both a physiological and biochemical adaptation, but this continual demand will ultimately drain the body of its resources and energy. When people begin to suffer from accumulated stress, they become susceptible to disease, particularly to psychosomatic ailments (Bloomfield, et al 1975). In our discussion of stress and the neurotransmitters (chapter 4), we observed that the disease mechanisms inherent in manic-depressive illness are very closely aligned with those pathways of the central nervous system that respond to stress. So while the rapid and incessant change of modern life effects every one of us, it will prove especially punishing for manic-depressives who have a genetic flaw impairing their capacity to cope effectively with stressful situations. Although the genetic research for manic depression is still in its very early stages, a very promising study by Dr. Dennis Murphy and others appeared in the November 29, 1996 issue of *Science* magazine. Murphy's findings suggest the genetic flaw involves the serotonin transporter gene regulatory region and this supports our focus on serotonin in chapters 4, 5, and 6.

Disturbed sleep is one of the most prominent effects of inordinate stress and, as we have carefully documented above, a consistent symptom of mental illness. In addition to sleeping pills and barbituates, the overindulgence in alcohol, cigarettes, marijuana, and cocaine is, in large part, a reaction to the destructive tendencies of too much stress in modern life — as is the increasing disaffection for work, for healthful kinds of recreation, and for a strong family unit.

What Is Meditation?

Significant numbers are now learning to cope with stress through meditation. Meditation is thousands of years old, but has only been studied in the West for its health benefits for the last 30 years. Unhappy with the side effects of drugs for stress-related disorders, health care workers welcome meditation as a means of reducing stress and an ever increasing number of both patients and doctors reap the health benefits of routine meditation.

Joan Borysenko, Ph.D. defined meditation as any "activity that keeps the attention pleasantly anchored in the present moment." When the mind is at peace and centered in the present, it is not worried about things past or preoccupied with future matters, two significant sources of persistent stress known to impair health. "Meditation," says Borysenko, "helps to keep us from identifying with the 'movies of the mind.'"

Meditation can be divided into one of two types: concentrative meditation and mindfulness meditation. Concentrative meditation works by centering the mind's attention on the breath, an image, or a sound (mantra), so as to quiet the thought processes and allow for increased clarity and alertness. This kind of meditation is analogous to the zoom lens of a camera that limits its focus to a specific field. Dr. Borysenko describes the second form, mindfulness meditation, as a process whereby the attention is opened "to a continuously passing parade of sensations and feelings, images, thoughts, sounds, smells, and so forth without becoming involved in thinking about them." The meditator remains quiet and merely witnesses what passes through his conscious mind, not reponding to or becoming involved with the images, memories, thoughts, or worries. This detachment helps the meditator attain a more serene, tranquil, and clear mental state. Whereas concentrative meditation is usefully compared to the zoom lens of a camera, mindfulness meditation is more akin to the wide-angle lens — a sweeping awareness that takes in the complete field of perception.

An Exercise in "Concentrative" Meditation

An initial step in learning concentrative meditation is to breathe in a way that allows a state of tranquility and alertness. The exercise described here is suggested by Jon Kabat-Zinn, Ph.D., Director of the Stress Reduction Clinic at the University of Massachusetts Medical Center as a particularly efficient manner of achieving a state of quiet and calm. Kabat-Zinn simply recommends you find a restful place where you will not be disrupted and do what follows for several minutes every day:

> Take a relaxed position sitting or lying on your back. If sitting, keep the back straight, and allow your shoulders to drop.
> If it contributes to your over-all comfort, gently close your eyes.
> Then, begin to center your attention on your stomach area and on its tendency to quietly expand and rise on the in-breath and fall or recede on the out-breath.
> Maintain this attention on your breathing, "being with" each in-breath.
> Each time you observe your thought-process moving away from the breath, focus on what it was that took you away and

gently bring the mind back to the stomach and the experience of the breath moving in and out.

Kabat-Zinn instructs that if the mind moves away from the breath, then it is the meditator's task to merely bring it back to the breath each time, no matter what thought has taken it away.

The idea is to practice this routine for just 15 minutes every day, whether you find it particularly appealing to do so or not, and just experience for one week what it is like to bring a disciplined meditation exercise into your life. See if it makes any difference to do nothing else for a few minutes each day but experience the ebb and flow of your own breath (Goldberg 1993).

Transcendental Meditation

Of the many variants of concentrative meditation (such as the breath exercise described above), Transcendental Meditation (TM) is the most thoroughly researched. TM is a simple, natural, and effortless technique that allows us to reach a restful state. It merely requires us to sit quietly and close our eyes for two brief periods each day. TM begins with the assumption that there are natural laws, that man is a part of nature, and that he would experience greater joy if he were more in tune with life's fundamental rhythms. If we were more aware of natural law, we would be better nourished, overcome stress and suffering, and move in the direction of a more refreshed and relaxed state of being.

Psychologists frequently tell us that man typically makes use of only 5-10% of his mental potential. Through the process of TM, we can attain the state of pure awareness — also called the field of silence or pure consciousness. By attaining this level, we are able to nourish the mind at its source, its reservoir. Allowing the mind to relax and settle down to this field of silence is analogous to watering a plant at its very roots. In order to revive the plant, it is not practical to nourish every one of its leaves — in the same way we nurture and revive the mind by allowing it to periodically visit this reservoir of pure consciousness.

By nourishing the mind at its source, then, we make it more efficient, more relaxed and alert, and allow the mind to access a greater degree of its own potential. Just as an archer must draw back the bow to thrust forward the arrow toward its target so too is it of great value to man to periodically bring the mind back to its source. If man is to act powerfully and efficiently, he must be capable of thinking clearly — and thinking has its ground in this reservoir of pure consciousness.

TM, if done properly, requires no effort. The technique involves sitting quietly for 15-20 minutes and allowing the mind to gradually quiet and settle itself. Just as we can move about at a variety of speeds depending on whether we run, jog, or walk, so too the mind can function at varying degrees of activity. When we sit down to meditate, our goal is to allow the mind to gradually decelerate the thought process until it reaches that degree of profound quiet where it actually transcends thought. Hence, the name given the technique, Transcendental Meditation.

As we sit quietly, the mind will begin to slowly decrease its activity and will naturally, of its own volition, gravitate toward this blissful state beyond or transcendent to thought. Man is taught, particularly in western culture, to develop the mind and to learn by projecting mind outward; we learn by studying what's external to us — by focusing the mind outward through the senses. Transcendental Meditation sometimes seems foreign to us initially because it essentially asks us to reverse that process. We are invited to rest the mind and to go within.

The TM theory rests on the assumption that mind and body are closely linked. As the mind slows down and attains its reservoir of healing, the body also experiences profound rest during this 15-20 minute period. The pace of modern life is so fast and there are so many demands on us we inevitably experience a build-up of stress and strain in our bodies. These short intervals of meditation, twice a day, actually achieve a more profound level of rest than do the most therapeutic levels of sleep itself; and, because so much of our insomnia is stress-related TM has been hailed as one of our best allies for improved sleep.

The TM technique dates back thousands of years through the Vedic tradition in India and the orient. From the earliest times, the meditation process has included the use of a specific sound, a mantra — the term is meant to suggest a sound whose effects are known to be good and to provide a life supporting effect on the nervous system. We all know there are sounds harsh and grating like the screech of fingernails on a classroom chalkboard or harmonious and pleasant like the gentle murmur of a bubbling brook in a quiet forest. This latter type of soothing, melodious sound that provides a positive, comforting effect facilitates every meditator as he or she experiences the rewards of this process. From ancient times these mantras or pleasant sounds have been passed down from teacher to student. Because it is believed each individual is unique and the thinking process is delicate and we all learn differently, each new meditator is given a special mantra. Accordingly, an experienced meditator will not train new meditators or assign mantras until he or she has received advanced training. Long-term meditators are very enthused about the benefits of the TM program and report its salutary effects increase over time.

Responsible research on the effects of TM suggests its particular appeal for manic-depressives. We observed in chapter 4 that abnormal amounts of cortisol secretion indicate stress; and, that studies report over 50% of manic-depressives show elevated cortisol levels (Sachar, 1982). Reporting in *Hormones and Behavior* for February of 1978, researchers Jevning, Wilson, and Davidson state, "We studied acute plasma cortisol and testosterone concentration changes during the practice known as 'transcendental meditation' (TM) and during control rest. Three groups of normal, young adult volunteers were studied: a group of controls, these same controls restudied as practitioners after 3 to 4 months of TM practice, and a group of long-term, regular TM practitioners (3 to 5 years of practice).

No change was found in controls during rest. Cortisol declined, but not significantly, in restudied controls, while cortisol decreased significantly in long-term practitioners during meditation and remained somewhat low afterward. . . . Apparently, the practice of TM becomes associated with psychophysiologic response(s) which acutely inhibit pituitary-adrenal activity." (*Hormones and Behavior,* Vol. 10, no. 1, Feb. 1978). These findings by Jevning, et al in their 1978 article were reenforced by Oliver R. Werner, et al in an article in 1986 entitled "Long-Term Endocrinologic Changes in Subjects Practicing the Transcendental Meditation and TM-Sidhi Program." The Werner study concludes, "The TM-Sidhi program may have marked longitudinal effects on pituitary hormone secretion. These findings are of particular interest in light of the reported beneficial effects of the Transcendental Meditation and TM-Sidhi program on mental and physical health and suggest that the TM-Sidhi program may be a very productive model for studying the relationship between subjective experience, health, and neuroendocrine function" (*Psychosomatic Medicine* Vol. 48, No. 1/2 (Jan./Feb. 1986).

In addition, a "meta-analysis," the preferred scientific procedure for drawing definitive conclusions from large bodies of research, found Transcendental Meditation produced a "significant increase in basal skin resistance compared to eyes-closed rest, indicating profound relaxation. Deep rest and relaxation were also indicated by greater decreases in respiration rates and plasma lactate levels compared to ordinary rest. These physiological changes occur spontaneously as the mind effortlessly settles to the state of restful alertness, pure consciousness." (*American Psychologist* 42: 879-881, 1987).

For more background on TM and further information on contacting a TM Center, see Robert Roth's helpful book entitled *Transcendental Meditation,* 1994. If meditation proves to be something that does not work for you, it can be extremely beneficial for manic-depressives to take a nap each day for 45 minutes or an hour just before or after supper. These daily naps are especially helpful when the sleep pattern is off, but for many bipolars a nap is beneficial on a regular basis. All of us benefit from a little additional rest, but this is particularly true of people with this illness.

Summary

Yes, there are occasions when none of these measures bring the desired sleep: not a sensible diet, not herbs, not exercise, not therapeutic baths, not meditation. And, we must keep in mind that some insomnia is not unhealthy; there are occasions when we are just too keyed up and excited to sleep. At those times, it is probably just as well not to fight it and get up and do something useful with that energy or just remain in bed and rest as quietly as possible. My mother's internist used to tell her that even though she didn't fall fully asleep, the body does benefit from just the rest — and, often, we sleep more than we think we do on such nights.

On the other hand, when we have tried a combination of the strategies outlined in this chapter and the problem seems to be the result of serious mania or depression — and it is on-going, we need to contact our psychiatrist or primary care physician, describe the problem, and begin taking the proper drugs for bipolar disorder. If we have already been diagnosed and we are on medication, it might be necessary to adjust our existing drugs, and/or — perhaps temporarily — take a prescription sedative. Manic-depressives must overcome problems with sleep as soon as possible.

8 Electroconvulsive Therapy

"We have witnessed a remarkable resurgence of interest in convulsive therapy in the past decade."

Max Fink, M.D., *Handbook of Affective Disorders*, 1992

U nfortunately many people associate electroconvulsive therapy, or "shock treatment" as it is commonly called, with a frightening portrayal of the procedure in a movie starring Jack Nicholson, "One Flew Over the Cuckoo's Nest." Though in the early days there was some justification for this expose, the treatment has been safe and humane for many years. I am personally very partial to ECT as it has revived my mother, an older brother, and myself from deep and persistent depressions. As we shall see, the research clearly supports ECT as a viable option for people with manic depression.

In the past many people dreaded these treatments, and ECT's potential for striking terror in the minds and hearts of patients and their families was not totally without reason. The first convulsive treatments were done without anesthesia or muscle relaxants, and for many patients they were experienced with fear and pain. Moreover, the notion of a consent form was still largely unheard of through the fifties and sixties — and patients were often treated against their will and without their formal consent. "One Flew Over the Cuckoo's Nest" did serve a positive purpose in symbolizing a general outcry against authority in the United States in the late sixties and focused specifically on this problem in psychiatry of administering ECT in an unfeeling and threatening manner. Finally, as a result of this film and many other political efforts, sufficient pressure was exerted on the American Psychiatric Association (APA) in the United States and the Royal College of Psychiatrists (RcPsych) in Great Britain to assure proper guidelines and standards were established for the use and treatment of ECT.

The Treatment Procedure

Of the many therapies and treatments available for depression and mania, ECT is probably the most involved and the one that most resembles surgery. ECT, therefore, usually requires a hospital setting. When one is emotionally sick it is expected almost any procedure will seem more of an ordeal, but I experienced shock therapy over thirty-five years ago and for me it was nothing to dread. I recall waking in the morning and taking an anesthetic. When the drug took effect, an electric current was passed through my brain. Several hours later I woke up feeling refreshed and two or three days later the procedure was repeated. I had 10 or 12 treatments over a period of three or four weeks. At the end of that time, I was nearly well. I could relax and smile and enjoy a meal for the first time in several months. I remained in the clinic for another three or four weeks, long enough to get my bearings and assess what had happened to me, and then returned home to a life of resumed purpose. With improvements in diagnosis and drugs and with today's pressures from insurance companies my stay in the clinic of 8-10 weeks back in 1961 would be reduced to just a week or two today; and, in some instances, the treatments can be started in the hospital and then completed as an outpatient or done totally on an outpatient basis.

For many years doctors believed ECT should be reserved for only the most acute and difficult depressions. ECT continues to be the treatment of choice for the most stubborn depression, but recent thinking favors its use in the following situations as well:

a) in a suicidal case, where a rapid, definitive response is required
b) when the risk of ECT is less than the risks of other treatments
c) when a patient (or his family) has not responded well to nutritional therapy, lithium, or the various anti-depressants but has a positive history with ECT
d) patient preference

Depression

Psychiatrists have found that drug response is sometimes dependent on families. Tricyclics and MAOI'S (monoamine oxidase inhibitors), for instance, can be very effective in lifting depression in some family groups but not in others. In some instances the seizure produced by ECT is the best answer. It is difficult to describe how completely debilitating, paralytic, and painful these bouts with acute depression can be. The loss of both parents, a sister, and my wife to cancer has been a source of much grief, but the emotion that accompanies these experiences does not approach the pain and despair one endures with a deep depression. The one is an emotional response to a life event; the other is the symptom of an illness: the two are vastly different.

Not all severely depressed patients are good candidates for ECT; e.g., it is not particularly beneficial for depression induced by neurosis — but for the endogenic manic-depressive whose illness involves the biochemistry its curative powers can border on the miraculous. Too many of the severely depressed endure endless suffering experimenting with the various anti-depressants when ECT (today a very safe, non-threatening procedure) is clearly the appropriate treatment.

Mania

Electroconvulsive therapy is effective with mania disorders as well. From its inception in the 1930's and extending through the first several decades of its use, ECT was shown to be very effective — even lifesaving — with manics (Max Fink, *Electroconvulsive Therapy*). And yet because of the dramatic results with lithium, ECT lost favor in treating mania. In the past decade, however, knowledge of patients who seem resistant to drug therapies and those who experience frequent and abrupt mood changes (known as "rapid-cyclers") has led to a re-evaluation of the role of ECT in treating manics.

Mode of Action

Convulsive Therapy was introduced in the 1930's based on the mistaken idea that epilepsy and schizophrenia do not occur together. If epileptics do not experience schizophrenia, it was assumed, it must be because of their periodic fits or convulsions. When convulsions were deliberately induced, however, researchers discovered while schizophrenics were somewhat improved the seizures were most helpful for the severely depressed. At first, fits or seizures were produced either by using cardiazol (Meduna, 1938) or by passing an electric current through the brain (Cerletti and Bini, 1938). Over the years, electrical stimulation became the procedure of choice. The subsequent addition of brief anesthesia and muscle relaxants made the treatment safe and acceptable.

For some time, even those researchers most involved with ECT were not entirely sure whether the passage of the current through the brain, the use of anesthesia and muscle relaxants, or the seizure itself actually produced the positive results associated with ECT. Clinicians are now generally convinced the patient does not improve unless a seizure is produced during the ECT procedure. This impression is strongly supported, though not proved beyond doubt, by the evidence of clinical trials. Thus less improvement is observed when the seizure is deliberately shortened by lidocaine (Cronholm and Ottosson, 1960) or when electric currents do not produce a full convulsion (Miller et al, 1953). There is also less improvement when the shock is left out but the anesthesia and all other aspects of the procedure remain the same (Brill et al., 1959; Robin and Harris, 1962; Freeman et al., 1978). So taken together, the general weight of evidence points to the importance of the convulsion. This conclusion is supported by the apparent therapeutic effectiveness of convulsions produced by the drug flurothyl, or Indoklon (Laurell, 1970, 1968).

By studying the effect of convulsions on animals (most specifically, rats), researchers believe they are beginning to understand what changes in the brain's chemistry are actually induced by the seizures. The action of the fit and its tendency to actually compress or "squeeze" operative centers in the brain causes an increased postsynaptic sensitivity to the neurotransmitters noradrenaline and dopamine (Gelder et al 1983). The action of these neurotransmitters has been linked to the neurotransmitter serotonin we discussed so thoroughly in chapter 4.

Undesirable Effects of ECT

Today, the use of lithium and the other increasingly more effective anti-depressant and anti-psychotic drugs — coupled with the laws requiring patient consent — make it unlikely a manic-depressive would be forced to endure electroconvulsive therapy under the adverse conditions of the past.

In the United States, three treatments of ECT a week is the standard compared to just two a week in Great Britain. Psychiatrists found early on that too many treatments over a short period of time is not effective and resulted in headache, nausea, and vertigo. In addition to spacing the intervals between treatments, the doctors have also learned if they apply the electrodes for passing the current to just one hemisphere (the non-dominant one) it is just as effective in inducing seizure and it is less apt to produce headaches. This unilateral placement of electrodes has also proven very beneficial in overcoming memory loss. The memory loss associated with ECT tends to be grossly exaggerated. At its worst, it involves a short loss of memory for events just prior to the procedure and impaired retention of information acquired soon after the treatment.

Deaths and ECT

The death rate attributable to electroconvulsive therapy was estimated to be 3-4 per 100,000 treatments by Barker and Barker in 1959. A recent survey of all ECT treatments given with anesthesia in Denmark, found a similar rate of 4 to 5 per 100,000 treatments (Heshe and Roeden

1976). The risks of death with ECT are related to the anesthetic procedure and are greatest in patients with cardiovascular disease. When death occurs it is usually due to ventricular fibrillation or myocardial infarction. So, the low number of deaths associated with ECT has more to do with general surgical conditions and poor health of the patient than anything inherently dangerous in the convulsion procedure itself.

Patient Consent and Legal Issues

Dating from its inception in the late thirties and extending through the first three or four decades of its use, controversy continued to surround electroconvulsive therapy. Medical legal language in both the USA and UK has been significantly changed now to protect the rights of the patient. The psychiatrists must pass through a number of steps before a patient's consent is given and the first treatment administered. For example, before a patient is asked to agree to ECT, it is essential to explain the procedure and indicate its expected benefits and possible risks (especially the possible effects on memory). The importance of this step is underlined by the finding (Freeman and Kindall, 1980) that only one-fifth of patients receiving ECT thought they had received adequate explanation. Many patients expect severe and permanent memory impairment after treatment and some even expect to suffer recurring fits. Once the doctor is sure the patient understands what he has been told, the latter is asked to sign a standard form of consent. The patient should understand that consent is being sought for the whole course of the procedure and not just one treatment (although he can of course withdraw consent at any time). All this is the doctor's job — he should not delegate it to other staff.

If a patient refuses consent or is unable to give it because he or she is in a stupor (or some other debilitating condition), and if — and only if — the situation is an emergency and the procedure is essential to save life, further steps are legally permissable according to Mental Health Acts in both the USA and UK.

9 The Case for Talk Therapy

"A cheerful heart is good medicine,
But a downcast spirit dries up the bones."

— Proverbs 17:22

For many individuals with bipolar disease, neurosis plays some role and it is just too simplistic to diagnose the disease as a biochemical disorder treatable by just nutrition and drugs.

When neurosis is suspected as a factor in manic-depressive symptoms, the patient must often consult more than one therapist. As we might expect, however, the therapists are more comfortable with and more partial to the discipline in which they had their training and have their greatest experience: psychiatrists are apt to believe drug therapy is the best approach, and the psychologists and social workers favor psychoanalysis and talk therapy.

Despite the philosophical differences between these professional groups, the better mental health clinics today feature both specialities in the same office and both offer invaluable expertise for the individual with bipolar disorder. Psychiatrists are schooled first as M.D.'s and

in the science of medicine: they are licensed to prescribe drugs and administer electroconvulsive therapy. Because bipolar disorder is, at
least to an important degree, genetic and biochemical and because so
much of mental and emotional disease is progressively treatable by
nutrition and drugs, a psychiatrist (a D.O. or an M.D.) is an absolute
must. At the same time, however, psychologists and social workers
trained in the psychological causes for emotional disturbance and in
therapies to help us cope with our emotions can be extremely effective
as well. Susan Dime-Meenan, executive director of the National Depressive and Manic-Depressive Association, clarified the relationship
of drug and talk therapy when she said, "It wasn't until I was on medication that I could start dealing with the emotional issues. Psychotherapy has helped me tremendously, but had the therapy preceded the
medication, I'd have been on the couch the rest of my life."

While a biochemical predisposition is observed in manic-depressives, it is equally true that as early as 1921 Kraeplin emphasized certain personality traits as precursive to this disease. Well known, respected, and highly successful psychologists like Aaron Beck have
argued for years that individuals who tend to worry and be unduly
apprehensive about life events — and to consistently think negative
thoughts have a far greater capacity for severe emotional illness.

The kind of emotional stress experienced by people who are subject to excessive worry and apprehension is too often ignored by a
mental health profession increasingly commited to drug therapy. Hans
Selye's theories on stress and the general adaptation syndrome suggest the need to combat these kinds of stressors by tapping the talent
and skills unique to the social workers and psychologists (talk therapists) as a very necessary complement to the work done by psychiatrists. If homeostasis and the "interieur milieu" are to be protected in
the interest of health, then it is only good sense to treat signs of emotional trauma.

When Selye calls for "homeostasis," he is asking for stability in
both the external environment and in the interior of the human organism. But the very nature of human life dictates our stability will be under constant seige. It is critical, therefore, that we understand the importance of "adaptation" in our efforts to attain "homeostasis." Those
with bipolar disorder experience this illness because physically and
emotionally their tools for adaptation are marginal. Since manic de-

pression involves the endocrine system (the hormones and neurotransmitters), we can improve adaptation biochemically through nutrition, drugs, meditation, exercise, and a myriad of other complementary treatments. Emotionally, social workers and psychologists improve adaptation through insightful analysis of psychic history and various therapies that enhance self-esteem and generally improve one's sense of well-being. But as Susan Dime-Meenan instructs us above, biochemical and emotional adaptation work together and complement one another. Her medication (the nutrition and drugs) produced the change that allowed her to benefit from talk therapy; and, the inverse is true as well: the insights and treatment afforded by the talk therapists reduce stress and conserve limited biochemical resources. The two forms of treatment work hand in glove and both are needed in the quest to best adapt and reach the optimum level of homeostasis and health.

Ego Psychology

In chapter 4 we described my first year at the university to illustrate the potential trauma during periods of transition for those especially vulnerable to stress. While the demands consistent with change along with my family history of manic depression provide sufficient cause for that attack my freshman year, the therapists who espouse ego psychology would find much to interest them in my case as well. It is customary to view ego psychology as evolving from classical psychoanalytic theory. Sigmund Freud laid the foundation for the contemporary study of the ego. His daughter Anna and Heinz Hartmann extended his views and helped make the theoretical leap that has initiated current views of ego functioning and development. Erik Erikson, Margaret Mahler, and Edith Jacobson have also made important contributions to this theory — as have many of the interpersonal counselors like Alfred Adler and Erich Fromm (Goldstein 1995).

These advocates of ego psychology would not deny the significance of my family history of manic-depressive illness, my biochemical tendencies, or the unique set of pressures I faced that first year at college, but they would find certain events in my psychic past equally compelling. For example, the fact that my mother experienced one of

119

her most severe and lasting depressions just after my birth and had to be hospitalized most of the first year of my life.

Erik Erikson viewed optimal ego development to result from the mastery of stage-specific developmental tasks and crises. He argued that the successful resolution of each crisis from birth to death leads to a sense of ego identity and may be said to constitute the core of one's sense of self. In *Childhood and Society* (1950) and *Identity and the Life Cycle* (1959) Erikson proposed that the human life cycle from birth to death could be conceived of as a series of eight successive stages.

According to Erikson, the foundation of all later personality development occurs in the first stage of the life cycle, in which the infant must develop a sense of basic conviction in the predictability of the world and its fulfillment of his or her needs:

> For the first component of a healthy personality I nominate a sense of basic trust, which I think is an attitude toward oneself and the world derived from the experience of the first year of life. By "trust" I mean what is commonly implied in a reasonable trustfulness as far as others are concerned and a simple sense of trustworthiness as far as oneself is concerned. . . . In adults the impairment of basic trust is expressed in a basic mistrust. It characterizes individuals who withdraw into themselves in particular ways when at odds with themselves and with others (Erikson, 1959:55-56).

The nature of the child's early interpersonal relationships is linked inextricably to stages in the evolution of internalized mental representations of others and of the self, both of which constitute the core of one's psychological identity. In other words, the child develops his or her sense of self and of others as a result of experiences with others. The inner representations of self and others, once developed, affect all subsequent interpersonal relations.

> It is helpful to . . . think in terms of the early mental processes by means of which the newborn infant organizes its world into meaningful patterns. One basic pattern is that of the self-representation while another is that of the object representation. The object refers to the primary mothering person or persons in the environment of the infant and the very young child.

Erikson believed the frustration of the infant's need to develop trust in this first critical stage of development could lead to problems with adaptation in subsequent stages and on into adult life. When my father learned mother's depression would involve many months in a sanitarium, he made other arrangements for my care — but the sense of trust Erikson finds so necessary in that infant stage might have been irreparably impaired. Erikson writes, "The main task of the caretaker is to attend to the child's needs in a way that is predictable and dependable." When my mother's enduring depression forced her to relinquish my care to others, some degree of trust was inevitably sacrificed; and, along with that lost trust, went certain healthy psychological predispositions. "Developing a sense of basic trust includes tolerating the unknown, learning the process of giving and taking without undue anxiety, and being able to explore the immediate environment without fear, dissatisfaction, or trauma. The child who acquires a sense of mistrust might at a later time show apprehensiveness and fearfulness, turn away from or against others, or reveal chronic depression, emptiness, fear of loss, or a sense of inner badness."

This analysis seems especially applicable to me. While I have strong attachments to my family and a few very good friends, my daughter has always teased me about "getting a life." She means that I have such a limited social life. Part of this is by design and not necessarily pathological as I have a great love for reading and choose to spend time alone for this reason. Yet, my daughter has a point, too, as I have always been somewhat ill-at-ease socially. I find it very difficult, for example, to relax with people in ordinary social situations: a cocktail party, a church picnic, or a class reunion. Because I can recall finding these kinds of situations difficult from my earliest days, I sometimes wonder if the basis of the problem doesn't emanate from these theories about early separation. I have also historically faced periods of change as exemplified by that traumatic first year at the university — with abnormal fear and apprehension. Accordingly, I might have benefitted from the intervention of a psychologist or social worker during those stressful transition periods of my youth and on into my adult life. An insightful and effective counselor could have helped me understand why I feel threatened by certain social situations and why periods of change are especially difficult for me. A talk therapist with expertise in ego psychology has a definite place in the treatment regimen for manic-depressives, but especially for an individual with my psychic past.

Separation theory such as espoused here in the work of Erik Erikson has been supported in animal studies for many years. Professor Harry Harlow, a behavioral psychologist at the University of Wisconsin, was doing significant research in separation theory with monkeys in the early 1930's. These separation models are based on the theoretical concept that humans and other animal species are in their most stable condition when they have secure social attachment systems and that disruption of these systems is very stressful.

The result of such disruptions is a development of grief reactions and, in some vulnerable individuals, these can serve as a risk factor for the development of clinical depressions. The reaction to separation is obviously influenced by many variables, including developmental, social and biological ones. Determining the influence of these variables and how they might interact with each other has been extremely difficult in humans and investigators have used animal paradigms to study the behavioral and, more recently, the neurobiological effects of separation.

In general, studies of mother-infant separation in primates are of two basic types. The first and by far the largest group of studies consists of research which experimentally separates the mother and infant in order to investigate the characteristics of the mother-infant relationship. Such studies have centered on the behavior of both mother and infant prior to, during and following a brief separation, or separations. While interpretation of data gathered in such studies may include reference to human mother-infant relationships, their focus has been on the assessment of the dyadic relationship of the monkeys rather than on the individual behaviour of one or the other. The second group consists of studies which have been conducted for the explicit purpose of 'modelling' human depressive disorders. These studies are much more limited in number than the mother-infant dyad studies and tend to involve permanent separations from mother, observational assessment of primarily the infant's behavior and assessment of biochemical or biophysiological variables in addition to behavior alterations.

A 1962 study by Jensen and Tolman separated two pig-tailed macaque infants aged 5 and 7 months from their mothers and then reunited the subjects with their own or the other subject's mother. They reported the separations as being highly stressful and accompanied by loud distress,vocalizations and arousal.

A number of other investigators subsequently have studied mother-infant separation in several primate species. For example, Seay et al (1962) separated rhesus macaques from their mothers at the ages of 5.5-7 months. These investigators, in agreement with Jensen and Tolman, reported that the separation was a highly traumatic event for both mothers and infants. The authors interpreted their data as being consistent with Bowlby's (1960) theory of primary separation anxiety and for the first time described the 'protest-despair' stages in non-human primate subjects. The 'protest' stage consists of disorientated scampering, high-pitched screeching and a general increase in activity levels. The 'despair' stage is characterized by decreased activity, vocalization, food and water intake, withdrawal and sometimes death.

Reite & Short (1978) have demonstrated that this latter stage in Macaca nemestrina (pig-tailed macaque) infants is accompanied by sleep EEG changes closely resembling those in human depression. Rhesus macaque infants who are undergoing the protest stage following maternal separation show an elevation of the enzymes involved in catecholamine synthesis as well as serotonin levels in the hypothalamus (Breese et al 1973). For further discussion of the studies cited here — and other investigations of the separation theory in animals — see Eugene Paykel's *Handbook of Affective Disorders*, 1992.

We make the point in various places earlier in this study that manic depression is, in large part, a biochemical disease handed down through the genes. We underscore this biochemical thesis when we suggest that most of older psychological theory — including much of Freud — is no longer relevant. Yet, we observe here in the ego psychology of Erik Erikson and the complementary studies on separation theory done on infant monkeys by Harlow, Jensen, Tolman, and others that certain psychic events in our past (sometimes behavioral and sometimes behaviorally-induced but also biochemical) need to be discovered, explored, and treated through psychotherapy and counseling as well as just pharmocology.

Cognitive Therapy

Cognitive therapists like Aaron Beck nicely complement the classical psychoanalysts and the proponents of ego psychology — in fact, in some ways the work of Beck and the cognitive school can be seen as an extension of the developments of Erik Erikson. The kinds of negative cognitions Beck worked so hard to overcome often have their origins in traumatic happenings during one or more of Erikson's eight psychosocial stages.

Beck proceeds from the assumption that the patient's thoughts may be the primary disorder, or at least very powerful factors in aggravating and perpetuating the disorder. He divides depressive cognitions (thought processes) into three components. The first is a stream of 'negative' thoughts, for example, 'I am a failure as a mother.' The second is a set of expectations, as in that a person cannot be happy unless everyone likes him. The third is a series of 'cognitive distortions,' of which four examples can be given: 'arbitrary inference,' drawing a conclusion when there is no evidence for it and even some against it; 'selective abstraction,' focusing on a detail and ignoring more important features of a situation; 'over-generalization,' drawing a general conclusion on the basis of a single incident; and 'personalization,' relating external events to oneself in an unwarranted way.

Beck would argue that a person who habitually adopts such ways of thinking will be more likely to become depressed when faced with a minor problem. For instance, a rebuff would be more likely to lead to depression in a person who thinks he needs to be liked by everyone, concludes arbitrarily that the rebuff means he is disliked, focuses on this event despite other evidence that he is generally popular, and draws these general conclusions from this single incident. (It can be seen from this example that the varieties of cognitive distortions are not entirely distinct from one another.)

It is very difficult to refute the theoretical basis of Beck's Cognitive Theory; viz., that negative thoughts produce negative feelings and emotions and Beck's assumptions have proven successful in working with neurosis and even to lengthen the period between attacks for persons with endogenous depression (Gath 1983).

Cognitive Therapy and Improved Compliance

Cognitive Therapists can also help manic-depressives in a more prag-
matic way by intervening with the tendency for non-compliance.
When the research clearly shows that lithium and the anticonvulsants,
carbamazepine (Tegretol) and valproic acid (Depakote), can relieve the
symptoms of bipolar disorder for the majority with the disease, it is vitally important we overcome the inclination to non-comply in taking
medications. In our discussion in chapter 6 of nutritional therapy's potential to help detoxify these drugs, we referred to the book, *Cognitive-
Behavioral Therapy for Bipolar Disorder*. In this publication, the authors
Monica Ramirez Basco, Ph.D. and A. John Rush, M.D. claim that up to
46% of those taking lithium fail to take their medication as prescribed.
Basco and Rush make the point that too often the failure to take medication as intended becomes a point of contention and strain between
the health practitioner and the patient. A major point of Basco and
Rush's particular speciality, Cognitive-Behaviorial Therapy (CBT), is
to move beyond the tendency to judge and blame the patient. Their
goal is to use education and the strategies of psychological intervention and talk therapy to help patients understand why they are remiss
in taking medication and what can be done to help them correct the
problem. After years of study and personal experience with bipolar
patients on lithium, Basco and Rush list what they call the "common
obstacles to adherence."

1. Intrapersonal variables.
   a. Remission in symptoms and seeing no need for further treat-
      ment.
   b. Decrease in energy, enthusiasm, creativity, and/or productiv-
      ity.
   c. Denial that they have a chronic illness/stigma associated with
      bipolar illness.
   d. Depressive relapse.

2. Treatment variables.
   a. Side effects of medication. (See b above).
   b. Medication schedule does not conform to patient's personal
      schedule.

3. Social system variables.
   a. Psychosocial stressors.
   b. Competing medical advice.
   c. Discouragement from family and friends.

4. Interpersonal variables.
   a. Poor rapport with the therapist and/or psychiatrist.
   b. Busy, uncomfortable, or otherwise unpleasant clinic environment.

5. Cognitive variables.
   a. Patient does not like the idea of having to depend on drugs.
   b. Patient thinks he or she should be able to handle mood swings on his or her own.
   c. Patient misattributes symptoms of bipolar illness to another source.

The attempt to overcome these obstacles to adherence has to begin with monitoring the degree to which the patient is taking the drug. There are many ways to deceive the doctor. For instance, the bipolar patient might be very casual in taking his or her dosage, but studies show if the correct dosage is taken for several days just prior to testing the blood lithium level, the test is apt to show a lithium level in the therapeutic range. When the patients are in the hospital or in a mental health clinic, the therapists can do spot-checks and overcome this kind of manipulation. But the majority of the time the patient is not hospitalized and the therapist must work with family members, friends, and with the patient to ascertain the level of compliance.

Basco and Rush use cognitive-behaviorial therapy to maximize the chance of adherence by minimizing the obstacles that interfere with the treatment plan. When there is a drug as effective as lithium for bipolar disease, the goal is consistency. CBT clinicians do not expect perfection in compliance; they are content with improvement. Some individuals will not comply simply because they associate medicine with illness and when they are not actually experiencing an attack of mania or depression they cannot convince themselves to take lithium as a preventative. In some instances, this type of bias and similar kinds of obstacles can be overcome through education. Seltzer,

Roncari, and Garfinkel(1980) provided nine lectures for inpatients on their diagnosis, course of treatment, medication, side effects, relapse, and importance of social support. Based on diagnosis and current medication type, 44 patients with schizophrenia, 16 with bipolar disorder, and 7 with major depression were placed in either education groups or a no education control group. Compliance was measured through pill counts or medication blood levels. Five months later, patients in the education groups demonstrated greater treatment adherence and were less fearful of side effects and drug dependency than were those in the control group. The non-compliance rate for educational group members was 9%, while the non-compliance rate for the control group was 66%.

While education can help many, the one-to-one give and take between therapist and patient is frequently needed to overcome the obstacles for compliance. Basco and Rush contend "the effective treatment of patients with bipolar disorder requires a long-term therapeutic relationship based on trust. Clinicians are often stabilizing forces in the lives of these patients." When a sufficient degree of trust is established between therapist and patient, the quality of communication improves. "In traditional physician-patient relationships, patients are expected to follow their physicians' instructions without question or complaint. In contrast, the cognitive-behavioral approach encourages patients to be informed consumers, which means asking questions, giving opinions, and feeling comfortable in disagreeing with clinicians. Active involvement in treatment helps patients to become invested in getting better. In a collaborative health care relationship, both parties are able to discuss the negative and the positive aspects of a treatment process" (Basco and Rush 1996).

The Art of Self-Referral

Too often we are unhealthy psychologically and suffer a high degree of stress because of a failure to know ourselves. Students in college or individuals in the working world frequently follow a course of study or pursue a career path because of societal pressures and not for reasons consistent with personal interests and goals. Rather than acting on our own beliefs and principles in an assertive and determined manner, we are too apt to stand by passively while others decide what is important to us or in our best interest. If this type of submissive behavior goes too far and is untreated, it can be as stressful and determinant in the onset of an attack of bipolar disease as any genetic or biochemical cause.

The widely read M.D., Deepak Chopra, makes the distinction between object-referral and self-referral. Object-referral means giving primary importance to externals instead of to oneself. The external might be an event, circumstance, thing, or a person. A person whose thinking is based on object-referral automatically assumes his mind has no influence over things in the outside world. A thought is a subjective event that ricochets around inside a mental bubble never able to break out. For all practical purposes, this means that object-referral awareness is mercilessly dominated by things. To illustrate his point, Chopra recalls a fable he used to hear in India as a young person growing up. "Once there was a poor villager who possessed only two things of any value — his son, who was sixteen, and a handsome gray pony. The villager loved these two above all else in creation. One day the pony vanished and could not be found. The villager was plunged into deep dejection. No one could lift his spirits until three days later, when the pony returned, followed by a handsome black Arabian stallion. Overjoyed, the man embraced the pony and quickly bridled the stallion.

His son eagerly asked if he could ride the wild horse, and since he could deny him nothing, the father consented. An hour later, news came that the boy had been badly thrown while riding on the beach. He was carried home in a litter, bruised and battered, his right leg shattered in two places. At the sight of his injured son, the father's happiness again turned to utter sorrow.

He sat in front of his hut wailing, when a contingent of the king's soldiers swept by. War was imminent, and their duty was to drag off conscripts from the village. They ruthlessly seized every eligible son, but when they came to this man's house, the soldiers saw that his son was maimed, and they left him behind. The father's tears turned to joy, and he gave fervent thanks to heaven for the tragedy he had bewailed the moment before.

What's peculiar about this fable is that it has no ending, and that is its moral. The rise and fall of the villager's spirits goes on and on, bound to the fate of a boy and a pony. In real life, people have more than two things they cherish, but the result is the same. So long as our happiness depends upon objects "out there," we are their prisoner. We have given our freedom away to things" (Chopra 1991).

Self-referral, Chopra explains, means we learn to assess reality not by things, people, and events "out there," but by our own feelings, instincts, and intuitions. If we begin to live by this principle of self-referral, "there is no mystery," writes Chopra, "when a shift in awareness causes a change in the body, because all reality begins with such a shift and keeps on changing as we do. Things appear to be happening to us, but in fact we are influencing the circumstances of our lives as they occur. If sufficiently alert, we could see our thoughts radiating like light from a candle or a star. Thoughts surge up from their invisible source and lap against the world like waves against the shore. They strike everything in our vicinity — oak trees, clouds, skyscrapers, other people, even the most random atoms and bits of atoms. These things are basically reflections seen in the mirror of our awareness, and the mirror is vast — our thoughts roll on as far as the edge of the universe, beginning, at a finite source but spreading out to infinity."

Mind-Body Connections

Although traditional medicine is far from prepared to admit that our thoughts play a major role in either the onset or the cure of disease, an increasingly impressive number of patients — and even some doctors — are open to the possibility. Michael Crichton, the popular author of *Jurassic Park* and other best sellers, shares an intriguing experience he had while training as a medical doctor at Harvard Medical School twenty-five years ago. Crichton remembers the months he spent on the cardiac ward of a Boston teaching hospital. It is, apparently, routine for third and fourth-year students to rotate briefly through all the major medical specializations. Crichton had no intention of pursuing cardiology, but he had a simple, quite novel insight during this particular rotation: what if heart disease was not the same for every patient but had some kind of personal meaning for each one?

In relating this experience in his autobiographical sketches titled *Travels*, Crichton writes, "Some time earlier, I had read about the practice of a Swiss physician who, in the 1930's, had taken a medical post in the Alps because it allowed him to ski, which was his great passion. Naturally, this doctor ended up treating many skiing accidents. The cause of the accidents interested him, since he was himself a skier. He asked his patients why they had had their accidents, expecting to hear that they had taken a turn too quickly, or hit a patch or a rock, or some other skiing explanation. To his surprise, everyone gave a psychological reason for the accident. They were upset about something, they were distracted, and so on. This doctor learned that the bald question, "Why did you break your leg?" yielded interesting answers.

So I decided to try that. I went around and asked patients. "Why did you have a heart attack?"

From a medical standpoint, the question was not so nonsensical as it sounded. During the Korean War, post-mortems on young men had shown that the American diet produced advanced arteriosclerosis by the age of seventeen. You had to assume that all these patients had been walking around with severely clogged arteries since they were teenagers. A heart attack could happen any time. Why had they waited twenty or thirty years to develop a heart attack? Why had their heart attack happened this year and not next, this week and not last week?

But my question "Why did you have a heart attack?" also implied that the patients had some choice in the matter, and therefore some control over their disease. I feared they might respond with anger. So I started with the most easygoing patient on the ward, a man in his forties who had had a mild attack.

"Why did you have a heart attack?"

"You really want to know?"

"Yes, I do."

"I got a promotion. The company wants me to move to Cincinnati. But my wife doesn't want to go. She has all her family here in Boston, and she doesn't want to go with me. That's why."

He reported this in a completely straightforward manner, without a trace of anger. Encouraged, I asked other patients.

"My wife is talking about leaving me."

"My daughter wants to marry a Negro man."

"My son won't go to law school."

"I didn't get the raise."

"I want to get a divorce and feel guilty."

"My wife wants another baby and I don't think we can afford it."

No one was ever angry that I had asked the question. On the contrary, most nodded and said, "You know, I've been thinking about that. . . ." And no one ever mentioned the standard medical causes of arteriosclerosis, such as smoking or diet or getting too little exercise."

In the late 1960s, the mind-body connection was considered not quite legitimate, and Crichton was perplexed by his patients' perspective. Looking back, he writes,"What I was seeing was that their explanations made sense from the standpoint of the whole organism, as a kind of physical acting-out. These patients were telling me stories of events and happenings that had effected their hearts in a metaphysical sense. They were telling me love stories. Sad love stories, which had pained their hearts. Their wives and families and bosses didn't care for them. Their hearts were attacked. And pretty soon, their hearts were literally attacked."

Crichton's experience as a medical student in a Boston teaching hospital and rumination about it deserves our thanks for anticipating a key mind-body concept, now more widely accepted, that our feelings do not live in a separate world from our cells. In his recent book, *Love and Survival*, Dean Ornish, M.D. writes, "At Yale, scientists studied 119 men and 40 women who were undergoing coronary angiography, an x-ray movie that shows the degree of blockages in coronary arteries. Those who felt the most loved and supported had substantially less blockage in the arteries of their heart. ...The wife's love and support is an important balancing factor which apparently reduces the risk of angina pectoris even in the presence of high risk factors" (Ornish 1998).

Finding Help for the Families

Included in this book are several references to my mother, and that is fitting because her experiences as a manic-depressive helped shape my understanding of this disease. But the dedication page for the study alludes to my father as well as my mother, and that is appropriate too for while dad did not have the illness he had to live with it for almost five decades.

I have little difficulty understanding what Michael Crichton is telling us above when he shares his interviews with heart attack victims and finds a mind-body connection. All I need do is relive my own father's experience with a heart attack. Quite regularly when my mother would swing to the mania pole of bipolar illness she became irritable and hostile; and, the target of her ire was inevitably dad. Throughout their nearly 50 years of marriage dad endured several of these manic swings and mother's extreme hostility. When they were in their mid-seventies, mother had still another of these venemous mood swings. Finally, my sister and I were called to their home to assist dad in having mother hospitalized. Dad was extremely distraught and weakened by mother's behavior and the thought he would have to lose her again to another stay in the hospital.

Within 24 hours of mother's admittance to the psychiatric clinic, dad admitted himself to a general hospital with severe chest pains. A week later, while still in the hospital, he had a massive coronary and died. Like Crichton's patients, dad's heart had been metaphysically and literally attacked. Though he had endured countless of these manic swings with mother and knew intellectually she was sick, she could be so convincing at these times a part of him was no longer sure she loved him. So it is not stretching it at all to affirm an attack of my mother's mania killed my dad.

We picked mother up at the sanitarium and drove her to the church the day of dad's funeral. Afterward, we drove her back to the institution. After 49 years of marriage, four children, and a good and productive life together, such an end. Talk about sad love stories.

I am sure in those years my mother lived following dad's death, she was forever grateful to my sister. That last afternoon at my parents' home when mother was so difficult and averse with dad and we were coaxing her to the car for the ride to the sanitarium, my sister had the presence of mind and goodness of heart to ask mother if she wouldn't give dad a hug good-by. Thank God, for a few brief moments the illness abated, and mother complied.

My parents' tragic end cries out for improved methods of teaching coping skills in families burdened with this disease. And this kind of help will not come from psychiatrists; they are simply not trained to provide it. It will have to come from psychologists and social workers. Just consider the frustrations and tensions this disease creates in families. My dad was an 8 to 5 person: he was home for dinner every night, never traveled with his work, and always placed his family first. He was steady and dependable, and I can never recall dad raising his voice. He had experienced mother's mood swings from the earliest days of their marriage, and for his day he had a clear understanding of the disease. On more than one occasion I can recall dad reassuring me that mother would soon get well — that her illness was merely the result of hormonal imbalance. Dad's understanding and his selflessness in patiently waiting out mother's moods was truly saint-like.

But it isn't only the help-mate, the care-giver torn apart in these relationships. Mother was manic-depressive yes, but she was also a caring, sensitive, and highly motivated individual who was at her best when mildly manic. While dad could see where these manic episodes were going, mother was determined to take advantage of the creativity and production these moods afforded and did not wish to be checked by him at every turn. In fact, the better he became over the years at sensing the swings the more difficult it became for her.

At times, the tension in my childhood home was palpable. My parents' contrasting personal make-up coupled with mother's volatile moods could make living with them a neurotic, unhealthy experience. Yet, despite their differences they clearly loved each other and the number one priority for both of them was without question the well-being of their four children. We felt we were at the center of our parents' lives, and they were such basically reasonable people they would have learned to manage the disease and allayed the tension in our home had help been available.

In my judgment, the kind of help our home so desperately needed is now on its way. David J. Miklowitz and Michael J. Goldstein (recently deceased) have published *Bipolar Disorder: A Family-Focused Approach*. Families like mine can benefit greatly from its many practical suggestions for improving communication and reducing tensions. For a book of its type, it is readily accessible and free of jargon. And yet, as valuable as this volume is as a direct read by the families themselves, the book is primarily designed to train professionals, psychologists and social workers, to effectively intervene with families. Dr. Miklowitz, a Ph.D. in psychology, trains his clinicians in family psychoeducation coaching them to approach all members of the manic-depressive family with the utmost sensitivity and respect as they confront an entire gamut of problems these families face regularly; e.g., control issues of denial and resistance such as we observed above with my dad and mother in determining how to respond to the onset of mood swing. Miklowitz and Goldstein are equally helpful with other interpersonal issues such as the challenge to resurrect trust pursuant to financial, sexual, and other damaging indiscretions that often accompany mania attacks.

Surely, if there is such a strong link from our thoughts and feelings to stress and the resulting disease states — as the evidence of Crichton and Ornish clearly suggests — we have an on-going need for the work of talk therapists. In spite of the growing body of research that underscores the significance of genetics and biochemistry, our own psychology determines a significant degree of our physical and emotional health. We gain significant benefits, then, from the intervention of the social workers and psychologists who have now developed any number of successful therapies to help us trace the source of emotional weakness in our psychic past, to generally improve our happiness and sense of well being through confronting our thought processes, and to relieve our tension through a variety of very effective stress reduction strategies.

10 Attitude

"To wish to be well
is part of becoming well."

— Seneca

Until the very recent past, studies show on average the number of
episodes in a manic-depressive's lifetime was 16 to 18 (Goodwin
and Jamison 1990). Research also suggests there seems to be a fairly
typical pattern for the illness. Interestingly, it starts out slowly: the average amount of time between the first and second episode is three
years; between the second and third, 2 years; between the third and
fourth, 18 months; and later episodes are spaced about 1 year. In addition, bipolars who exhibit certain risk factors (severe mania, rapid cycling, mixed states, and evidence of substance abuse) have a less optimistic prognosis.

Today's advanced therapies, however, render these earlier pre-
dictors much less threatening. As we observed in chapter 6, even those
individuals with high risk factors and a poor outlook have been significantly helped by the drugs, Tegretol and Depakote, and now an im-

proved third generation of these anti-convulsant drugs is available. The truth is that nature and science have been most generous in providing non-prescription and prescription medicines for practically every conceivable kind and degree of affective disease. So if a manic-depressive seeks professional help, he or she should find a significant measure of relief.

But success in controlling bipolar disease is not strictly determined by genetic factors, biochemistry, or the latest designer drugs. It also depends on one's personal environment, on the persons and conditions which influence opportunity, character, and personality. Pete Harnisch, a major league pitcher with the Cincinnati Reds, experienced a severe depression in 1997 while pitching for the New York Mets and went on the disabled list. Because he is blessed with a supportive and nourishing family and friends, ample financial resources, and an essentially healthy ego, we are not surprised that Harnisch is fully recovered and back pitching for Cincinnati.

Unfortunately, not every individual who must fight manic-depressive illness does so with the same set of advantages. Either because they have a genetic make-up especially vulnerable to the disease, a singularly difficult "personality factor" such as we observed in chapter nine — or because they lack the emotional support or financial resources of a Pete Harnisch, these individuals are ill-equipped to fight this disease. The barriers unique to these people present enough of an obstacle, but then lead to problems with attitude as well. Many in this group, as we have said, benefit from extensive talk therapy and psychoanalysis and this is why it is so vitally important insurance companies and county and state funded agencies be encouraged to provide more generous coverage in this area. This group needs to explore their own behavior with the help of a professional psychologist until they discover why they seem determined to do themselves in. The problem is not that a regime like supernutrition, drugs,and regular talk therapy has failed to stabilize their moods, but simply that some of these individuals refuse to sufficiently discipline themselves to follow such a regime.

When personal and financial resources are at a minimum, we can almost predict an attitude marked by discouragement and denial. Denial can be a reality with any disease. People with lung and heart disease know they have alarming symptoms but fail to see a doctor and stop smoking. The family of an alcoholic becomes an enabler rather than confront the issue and demand the user seek help. Even individuals with diabetes will deny the seriousness of their disease before following a much needed special diet or drug regimen. If these other illnesses are subject to denial, it is not at all surprising that people who are manic-depressive have difficulty facing their disease: there is still a unique stigma attached to mental illness in our society and it is natural an individual would disavow it.

Although denial is very understandable, manic-depressives must quickly get beyond it and accept their condition. They must measure the illness against other positive aspects of their lives, and building on these other strengths, create a healthy, happy existence. But the high percentage who fail to comply with their medication indicates denial is a difficult barrier to overcome. In chapter four when trying to assess the causes for my second severe attack as a freshman in college, I alluded to the fear I would be locked away again as I was with my initial attack at fifteen. For me, denial involved the horror of being confined against my will; others might be haunted by memories of jail, court, or the extreme embarrassment of past manic behaviors. Most of us who have been manic recall a family member or dear friend to whom we have inflicted great pain when we said or did something while clearly out of control and not ourselves. No one wants to accept that their behavior so offended another human being that it led to a prolonged, or in some instances, a permanent division. That is a very difficult burden. Yet the guilt of these memories must be confronted and overcome lest the manic-depressive be incapacitated and paralyzed indefinitely. Frozen by these and a multitude of other reasons for denial, we fail to constructively manage the illness.

We cannot allow the hopelessness to get us. We must remind ourselves that all people, not only those affected by mental illness, experience sickness and loss. We must remember, too, even in our darkest hours, that manic depression is a periodic disease; and, in spite of the statistics we cite above concerning numbers of episodes over a lifetime, average time-lapse between attacks, or poor outcome risk factors, we now have the knowledge and medicines to attain remission much of the time. We are especially encouraged when we recall that many individuals with manic depression did extremely well even before the breakthroughs in medicine of the past twenty-five or thirty years. By studying the lives of these people we get a true picture of the course this illness can take over the period of a long life — without drugs complicating the issue. As desperately sick and depressed as members of these earlier generations were at times, they often lived active, happy, and productive lives — sometimes for seven and eight decades. And, in many instances, a history of their illness will reveal they only required three or four years of total hospital time over a life span of many years. So we can be positive about the illness knowing it is cyclic and simply make it our challenge to extend the time-line between attacks as far out as possible.

Habit and Discipline

Those with severely flawed genes, personality disorders, and inadequate support definitely face a steeper path with this disease than others. And yet, even these less fortunate can take encouragement from our parents and grandparents. Prior to the revolution in drugs, our ancestors often returned from sanitariums with a buoyant outlook ready to do battle with the world again. These earlier generations were forced to rely on something other than designer drugs and insightful psychotherapists; they teach us that a measure of optimism, determination, and common sense can go a long way in helping to regain one's health and well-being.

But the positive outlook and iron-clad will these hardy predecessors exercised in confronting bipolar illness was acquired over time. People do not suddenly will themselves to combat adversity. Will is a by-product of one's character and habits. We gradually acquire this virture step-by-step, through a number of small gestures and disciplined decisions. When we know a disease is exacerbated by irregular sleeping and eating habits, frustrating work, a failure to regularly attend counseling sessions and take medications, immoderate drinking and smoking, abuse of drugs, and other stressful pursuits, it is imperative we learn to make the little, tough decisions that in the aggregate insure our growth and health.

The eminent physician and psychologist of Harvard University, William James, discussed character in terms of habit and will in *The Principles of Psychology*. What he says is directed overtly at young people but applies to all of us at any age. James writes, "The physiological study of mental conditions is thus the most powerful ally of hortatory ethics. The hell to be endured hereafter, of which theology tells, is no worse than the hell we make for ourselves in this world by habitually fashioning our characters in the wrong way. Could the young but realize how soon they will become mere walking bundles of habits, they would give more heed to their conduct while in the plastic state. We are spinning our own fates, good or evil, and never to be undone. Every smallest stroke of virtue or of vice leaves its never so little scar. The drunken Rip Van Winkle, in Jefferson's play, excuses himself for every fresh dereliction by saying, 'I won't count this time!!' Well, he may not count it, and a kind Heaven may not count it; but it is being counted none the less. Down among his nerve-cells and fibers the molecules are counting it, registering and storing it up to be used against him when the next temptation comes. Nothing we ever do is, in strict scientific literalness, wiped out. Of course, this has its good side as well as its bad one. As we become permanent drunkards by so many separate drinks, so we become saints in the moral, and authorities and experts in the practical and scientific spheres, by so many separate acts and hours of work."

Are we saying, then, that emotional illness is, in the end, just a character flaw — that if we are just tough enough and sufficiently disciplined we can overcome it? Absolutely not: this entire study has emphasized the role of genetics, biochemistry, and very real neurosis. No, we are not saying this condition is fundamentally a matter of character, but we are affirming that manic-depressive illness is like any other obstacle or challenge in life. It is not just the fact it is there, but what we decide to do about it.

Sometimes when stiff competition is present as in a political campaign, auditions for a coveted role in a film or play, or an athletic contest, we talk about the importance of "heart." The candidate or performer who wins the day is not always the one with the most talent, but rather the one with this intangible we call heart. It is this aspect that stands at the innermost core of our personal (one might even say spiritual) reality. Philosopher Dallas Willard claims it is this heart or will "that organizes all the dimensions of personal reality to form a life or a person. [It] is the executive center of the self." The people we admire the most in life are those that demonstrate creative leadership.

"We always place a tremendous premium on what comes from the center of our being, the heart. It, more than anything else, is what we are."

In assessing the various roles of good luck, affluence, intelligence, and strength in making us "feel ourselves a match for life," William James adds, — "but deeper than all such things, and able to suffice unto itself without them, is the sense of the amount of effort which we can put forth. This effort seems to belong to an altogether different realm, as if it were the substantive thing which we *are,* and those were but externals which we *carry.* Our consents or non-consents seem our deepest organs of communication with the nature of things! What wonder if the effort demanded by them be the measure of our worth as men . . . the one strictly underived and original contribution which we make to the world!" (Willard 1998).

Statements by Melanie Branch and Stephen Szabo, both bipolar patients of career psychiatrist Peter Whybrow, seem to be reaching toward what Willard and James are defining here as our "executive center." In a presentation before Professor Whybrow's neuroscience class, Melanie asserts, "There is no magic bullet for these illnesses. The hardest and most important lesson to be learned is that the answer is not to be found in a pill bottle. This is not to say that medications are not helpful," she added. "In my case they have provided me with the necessary stability and relief to move ahead and take care of myself. But they are a tool I use to make a better life." Stephen Szabo echoes Melanie's experience with the disease when he states, "Assuming biology to be the only significant part of the puzzle, as I did for several years and especially after I agreed to try lithium, implies certain things about treatment — it's like the promise of a biological silver bullet. It makes it too easy for patients to take themselves off the hook of personal responsibility and to behave like victims, which is not healthy in the long run. I see it as similar to taking insulin for diabetes and then ignoring the need for an appropriate diet.

"And the same holds true in reverse, at least for an illness like mine. Psychotherapy by itself is not the answer. You can't think your way out of mania. I know; I've tried. The secret to successful self-care is a combination of pharmocology and self-knowledge. Medicine remains an empirical science. It's too early to build monuments to simple solutions to chronic illness, whether the disorder is diabetes or manic depression. This illness has taught me to respect the pluralism of science, in medicine at least, but it has also taught me that there is no substitute for personal responsibility and intelligent pragmatism when it comes to caring for oneself" (Whybrow 1997).

Taking Hold

When Stephen Szabo urges us to take personal responsibility, he means we have to take an active role in helping to manage our own illness. In the early stages this will be difficult because we have so much to learn. A physician who schedules us in once every six weeks or once a month to supervise our medication is not providing sufficient care. In addition to the psychiatrist prescribing our medication, we need a psychologist or other mental health therapist (especially in these early stages, but for most of us on an on-going basis) who is very knowledgeable in our specific illness. Someone who will see us frequently, educate us in the illness, provide feedback on our symptoms and behavior, and just generally offer the psychotherapy that will help us combat the multitude of stressors we have shown to be an integral part of the illness.

But there are organizations, associations, and support groups in place to assist us in the learning process as well. An important early step is to contact the National Depressive and Manic-Depressive Association (the DMDA at 800-826-3632 or www.ndmda.org) and ask to subscribe to their newsletter. They will help identify a local group for manic-depressives as it is important we develop a close support system. An illness that effects the emotions and mind is not something that can be handled well alone. We need sympathetic people who can assist us in getting to a doctor's office when we are too sick to accept we are sick or too depressed to care about help. Some of us have a built-in inertia to seeking help: we must overcome it.

These local chapters of DMDA can be very helpful; it is of great value to interact with others who have the illness. They might have more experience with the disease and be in a position to share important insights — information that will save not only time and money but unnecessary suffering. My own local chapter of DMDA meets twice a month for two hours in the evening. We typically have a group of thirty or thirty-five: most of these are people with the illness, but a spouse, parent,or close friend will typically show up as well to learn all they can. We meet for one hour with everyone, then break into smaller groups of 6 to 8. In the larger group, we might have a guest speaker; for example, someone representing the community health system who is anxious to share information and field questions on mental health programs or we might invite a labor attorney to discuss the respective rights of employers and employees in questions of disability and "reasonable accommodation." Or, on those occasions when we haven't scheduled a speaker we will discuss issues unique to those with the illness; such as, the need for political support for mental health legislation.

In the more intimate small group setting, no one is asked or compelled to share — but we find these groups non-threatening and we often give a history of our personal experience with the illness. This can be very helpful as we discuss specific symptoms — often behaviors that might be considered embarrassing and not easily shared in a less empathetic group. Swapping stories about medications can be beneficial as well: we learn of new drugs that prove more effective with less severe side effects or that doctors often get better results when they use combinations of drugs. We also discover we are not all the same biochemically — and a drug effective for one might not be for the next person. Sometimes, we just sit together as friends and discuss any issue of the day that might interest us. But whatever direction the conversation takes on a given night, everyone seems to enjoy the process and we leave feeling much better.

In addition to the interaction afforded by a local chapter of DMDA, these periodic meetings can also provide a rich source of written informaton on depression and manic depression. At each meeting a sub-committee of our chapter provides several hand-outs on any number of issues relevant to managing the disease. Browsing through these articles can be extremely helpful. As I have said elsewhere in these pages, we need to keep informed and provide meaningful input in sessions with our doctors.

Stephen Szabo's caveat we assume personal responsibility also implies we find the right doctor and medication. Persistence is the key. With all the advancements in nutritional knowledge and psychotropic medications, we can be reasonably confident the medicines are available to make us feel better. If, after repeated trials, we are certain the medications are not available, we need to accept the degree of wellness our particular illness and treatment will permit for now. And have faith, new treatments and medications are in the pipeline.

Medical research will soon provide the drugs and treatments for those still in need, and very likely, unravel the remaining genetic implications for manic depression as well. For the vast majority, however, we know enough today to bring affective disease to its knees if only we have the personal will. But the kind of effort and will we are asking here of manic-depressives is not unlike that of recovering alcoholics. Such effort necessitates a deep sense of security, an inner well-being that compels the patience and loving concern of family, friends, and wise and able doctors. And a knowledge that real healing entails a spiritual dimension as well as the physical and psychological.

Appendix A: Meals High In Serotonin

[These suggestions for achieving a diet high in serotonin are taken from *The Serotonin Solution* by Judith Wurtman, Ph.D. For a full discussion of the importance of serotonin in the diet and a vast array of menu suggestions for breakfast, lunch, and dinner, see Ms. Wurtman's book.]

Breakfast Exchanges
2 protein (16 to 18 grams)
1 starch (15 grams)
1 fruit (15 grams)
total calories: 280

To achieve a breakfast with this combination of proteins, starches, and fruits, Ms. Wurtman suggests a yogurt-fruit sundae (1 cup fat-free sugar-free yogurt mixed with one-half cup fat-free ricotta, 3 tablespoons Grape-Nuts sprinkled on top, with three-fourths cup fresh berries or one-half banana, sliced) or 1 egg cooked any style (if fried or scrambled use nonstick spray), 1 turkey sausage, one-half English muffin, and 1 teaspoon jelly.

Lunch Exchanges
3 protein (24 grams)
2 starch (30 grams)
2 vegetable (10 grams)
1 condiment and "free" food
total calories: 420

Ms. Wurtman insists we can achieve these ideal proportions of protein, starch, and vegetables at lunch time by returning to old lunch staples. We should eat canned tuna, turkey and chicken cold cuts, mock crabmeat, nonfat cheese, frozen vegetable mixtures (which can be thawed and mixed into the starchy component of the meal), and even microwaveable soups. She recommends we buy peeled, cut-up vegetables or if we have access to a salad bar or a restaurant that sells salads or an assortment of raw or cooked vegetables, we can get our selection there. We can bring the protein from home and add to it.

Dinner Exchanges
1 protein (8 grams)
3 starches (45 grams)
2 vegetable (10 grams)
1 fruit (15 grams)
2 fat (10 grams)
total calories: 510

To attain this high carbohydrate dinner, Ms. Wurtman offers the following sample dinner menus:

two 6-inch pancakes or two slices of French toast
1 tablespoon lite pancake syrup
one-half cup nonfat cottage cheese
1 cup chopped melon
Equals: 1 protein, 3 starch, 1 vegetable, 1 fruit

or

1 large baked potato stuffed with 1 ounce turkey or chicken (leftover or

part of family dinner) and one-half cup salsa, warmed
1 cup strawberries
1 cup steamed spinach tossed with 1 teaspoon olive oil
2 cinnamon WASA crackers
Equals: 1 protein, 3 starch, 1 fruit, 1 fat

Appendix B: Foods High in Tryptophan

[I provide below a list of the foods particularly high in the amino acid, tryptophan. Tryptophan is important not only because it is an "essential" amino acid but also because it functions as a precursor to serotonin. For a complete list of foods and their respective amounts of tryptophan, see Kirschmann and Kirschmann, *Nutrition Almanac, Fourth Edition.*]

Food	Measure	Weight	Mgs. of Tryptophan	Calories
Cereals				
cooked oatmeal	1c	234 gms	82	145
Dairy				
low fat cottage cheese	1c	226 gms	346	203
processed swiss	1oz	28 gms	102	95
milk, lowfat 2%	1 c	244 gms	115	121

Fish

Flounder, baked	3.5 oz	100 gms	300	202
Grouper, boiled	3 oz	85 gms	236	100
Perch, baked	3 oz	85 gms	236	99
Salmon, pink, cooked	3 oz	85 gms	189	118
swordfish, baked	3 oz	85 gms	241	132
Tuna, water packed	3 oz	85 gm	277	111
Whitefish, cooked	3 oz	85 gms	223	92

Legumes

Great Northern	1 c	177 gms	475	210
Soybeans, cooked	1 c	172 gms	416	298

Meats

Chuck Roast	4 oz	113.5 gms	395	224
Ground Beef, lean, broiled	3.5 oz	100 gms	305	272
liver	4 oz	113 gms	397	183
Sirloin Steak	4 oz	114 gms	231	295
Turkey, breast meat	1 slice	21 gms	54	23

Nuts

Almonds, dry roasted	1 oz	28 gms	83	167
Peanuts, oil roasted	1 oz	28 gms	92	161
Soybeans, dry roasted	.5 c	86 gms	495	387

Poultry

chicken, light w/o skin, roasted	3.5 oz	100 gms	361	173
Turkey, light w/o skin roasted	3.5 oz	100 gms	340	157

Appendix C: Physical Illness and Manic Depression

In accordance with Hans Selye's general adaptation syndrome and its concept of nonspecific stressors it follows that any physical illness can impact the endocrine system and help induce affective disorder. Some illnesses, however, seem particularly prone to bring on depression; for example, influenza, glandular fever ("mono"), hypoglycemia (low blood sugar), Parkinsonism, and puerperum (though this last connotes the six-month period following child birth and not a disease).

In addition, a whole gamut of diseases that involve the endocrine system directly and are characterized by either the overproduction of a specific hormone (hyper) or the underproduction of that hormone (hypo) can very closely resemble the symptoms of manic-depressive illness. Any individual thought to have a number of the symptoms consistent with either depression or mania as outlined in Chapter 3 should be checked for the following illnesses as they might be contributing to actual manic depression or merely mimicking the symptoms.

Hyperthyroidism

In hyperthyroidism (an oversecreting thyroid gland) there are always some psychological symptoms, including restlessness, irritability, and distractibility, which may be so marked as to resemble anxiety neurosis. In the past, acute organic psychiatric syndromes were observed as part of a 'thyroid crisis', but with modern treatment they are rare. Mild degrees of memory impairment can often be demonstrated if specifically sought (Whybrow and Hurwitz — 1976).

Hypothyroidism

Lack of thyroid hormones also invariably produces mental effects. In early life, it leads to retardation of mental development. When thyroid deficiency begins in adult life, it leads to mental slowness, apathy, and complaints of poor memory. These effects are important to psychiatrists because they easily lead to a mistaken diagnosis of depressive disorder.

In determining the cause of hypothyroidism, it is important to remember that lithium therapy might be a cause. See the Whybrow, Hurwitz 1976 study and *Hypothyroidism: The Unsuspected Illness* by Broda O. Barnes, M.D., 1976.

Addison's Disease (Hypoadrenalism)

Psychological symptoms consistent with under-producing adrenal glands are withdrawal, apathy, fatigue, and mood disturbance. Addisonian crises are almost always accompanied by the features of an acute organic psychiatric syndrome. The diagnosis is usually apparent because the patient is obviously unwell, cold, and dehydrated, with low blood pressure and signs of failing circulation. Occasionally a severe depresssive or schizophrenic picture coincides with Addison's disease, but less commonly than in Cushing's syndrome.

Cushing's Syndrome (Hyperadrenalism)

Emotional disorder is common, as Cushing noted in his original description. Cushing's disease usually comes to attention because of physical symptoms and signs, and any psychiatric disorders are usually encountered as complications in known cases. The physical signs include moon-face, 'buffalo hump', purple striae of the thighs and abdomen, hirsutes, and hypertension. Women are usually amenorrhoeic and men often impotent.

Depressive symptoms are the most frequent psychiatric manifestations of Cushing's syndrome. Paranoid symptoms are less common and appear mainly in patients with severe physical illness (Cohen 1980; Starkman and Schteingart 1981). The psychological symptoms usually improve quickly when the medical condition has been controlled. A few patients develop a severe depressive disorder with retardation, delusions, and hallucinations. Even these severe disorders generally improve when the endocrine disorder is brought under control.

Hypopituitarism

Psychological symptoms are usual. From a survey of the literature, including his own series of cases, Kind (1958) concluded that 90 per cent of patients with hypopituitarism had some psychological symptoms, while half had severe symptoms. The main symptoms were depression, apathy, lack of initiative, and somnolence. Psychological symptoms usually respond well when hypopituitarism is treated by replacement therapy.

Hyperparathyroidism

Psychological symptoms are common and apparently related to the raised blood level of calcium consistent with this disease. In two reported series (Petersen 1968; Karpati and Frame 1964) depression, anergia, and irritability were the most frequent symptoms. A few patients first present with psychiatric symptoms, while many patients re-

151

port, in retrospect, that they had experienced low spirits for years before definite symptoms appeared.

Hypoparathyroidism

Hypoparathyroidism is usually due to removal of or damage to the parathyroid glands when the thyroid gland is removed — on occasion, however, the cause is not surgical but just body chemistry. Though it is not a common symptom with this disease, there are instances of depression, irritability, and nervousness. Manic depressive and schizophrenic disorders are rare and may be coincidental. The diagnosis is made on the basis of physical symptoms (spasms of face, hand, and feet muscles; ocular cataracts; epilepsy) and measurement of serum calcium.

Mania And Physical Disease

Along with these many physical diseases of the endocrine system that either contribute to or mimic the symptoms of depression, mania has been reported in association with other physical illnesses (for example neoplasm and virus infections), medications (notably steroids), and surgery. [See Krauthammer and Klerman (1978) for a review of this evidence on mania and physical illness] (Gath 1983).

References

Chapter One

5   Price, J. "The genetics of depressive behaviour." In *Recent developments of affective disorders. British Journal of Psychiatry* Special Publication No. 2 (ed. A. Coppen and S. Walk), 1968.

5   Bertelsen, A., Harvald, B., and Hauge, M. "A Danish twin study of manic-depressive disorders." *British Journal of Psychiatry* 130, 330-351, 1977.

5   Mendelwicz, J. and Rainer, J. D. "Adoption study supporting genetic transmission of manic-depressive illness." *Nature* 268, 327-9, 1977.

5   Fieve, Ronald R., M.D. *Moodswing.* New York: Bantam Books, 1989, pg. 34-35.

Chapter Two

7   Burton, Robert. "The Anatomy of Melancholy" in *17th Century English Prose,* edited by David Novarr. New York: Alfred A. Knopf, 1967, pg. 89.

8   Kraepelin, E. *Manic Depressive insanity and paranoia* (translated by

R. M. Barclay from the 8th Edition of *Lehrbuch der Psychiatrie*, Vols. III and IV). E. and S. Livingstone, Edinburgh. 1921.

10   Basco, Monica Ramirez, Ph.D., and Rush, A. John, M.D. *Cognitive-Behavioral Therapy for Bipolar Disorder*. New York: The Guilford Press, 1996, pg. 206.

Chapter Three

12   Dunner and Colleagues (1976) & Angst (1978) in Goodwin, Frederick K., M.D., and Jamison, Kay Redfield, Ph.D. *Manic-Depressive Illness*. New York: Oxford University Press, 1990, pg. 64.

14   Schou, Mogens. *Lithium Treatment of Manic-Depressive Illness*. Basel: Karger, 1993, pg. 7.

17   Jamison, Kay Redfield, Ph.D. *Touched With Fire*. New York: The Free Press, pg. 140.

28   Fieve, Ronald R., M.D. *Moodswing*. New York: Bantam Books, 1989, pg. 109 and 202-203.

Chapter Four

30   Kelsoe, John R., M.D. "The Genetics of Bipolar Disorder." *Psychiatric Annals* 27: 4/April 1997.

31   Selye, Hans, M.D. *Stress Without Distress*. New York: Signet Books, 1974, pg. 26.

33   Whybrow, Peter C., M.D. *A Mood Apart*. New York: Basic Books, 1997, pgs. 8-10.

40   Sachar, E. J., Puig-Antich, J., and Ryan, N. D., et al. "Three Tests of Cortisol Secretion in Adult Endogenous Depression." *Acta Psychiatrica Scandinavica* 71: 1-8, 1985.

42   Holsboer, F., 1983; Holsboer, F., et al. 1984c, 1985. "The Hypothalamic-Pituitary-Adrenocortical System," in Paykel's *Handbook of Affective Disorders*, 2nd edition, 1992.

44   Heninger, G. R., et al. "Serotonergic Function In Depression: Prolactin Response to Intravenous Tryptophan in Depressed Patients and Healthy Subjects." *Arch Gen Psychiatry* 41: 398-402, 1984.

44   de'Montigny, C., et al. "Lithium Carbonate Addition in Trycyclic Anti-depressant-resistant Unipolar Depressions: Correlations with the Neurobiologic Actions of Tryclic Anti-depressant Drugs and Lithium Ion on the Serotonin System." *Arch Gen Psychiatry* 40: 1327-1334, 1983.

45   Meltzer, H. Y., et al. "Effect of 5 — hydroxytryptophan on Serum Cortisol Levels in Major Affective Disorders: I. Enhanced response in depression and mania." *Arch Gen Psychiatry* 41: 366-374, 1984.

45   Fuller, R. W. "Serotonergic Stimulation of Pituitary-Adrenocortical Function in Rats." *Neuroendocrinology.* 32: 118-127, 1981.

46   Prange, A. J., Jr. "L-tryptophan in mania: Contribution to a Permissive Hypothesis of Affective Disorders." *Arch Gen Psychiatry* 30: 56-62, 1974.

46   Kety, S. S. "Brain Amines and Affective Disorders." In *Brain Chemistry and Mental Disease.* William McIsaac, editor. New York: Plenum Press, 1971, pp. 237-263.

46   Mandell, A. J., and Knapp, S. S. "Asymmetry and Mood, Emergent Properties of Serotonin Regulation." *Arch Gen Psychiatry* 36: 909-916, 1979.

47   Born, J., et al. "Differential Effects of Hydrocortisone, Fluocortolone, and Aldosterone on Nocturnal Sleep in Humans. *Acta Endocrinologica* 116: 129-133, 1987.

Chapter Five

52   Davis, Adelle. *Let's Get Well.* New York: Penguin Books, 1987, pps. 22 - 31.

54   Balch, James F., M.D., and Balch, Phyllis A., C.N.C. *Prescription for Nutritional Healing.* Garden City Park, New York: Avery Publishing Group Inc., 1990, pg. 237.

55   Goldberg, Burton. *Alternative Medicine: The Definitive Guide.* Fife, Washington: Future Medicine Publishing, Inc., 1993, pg. 24.

55   Wurtman, Judith J., Ph.D. *The Serotonin Solution.* New York: Fawcett Columbine, 1996, pps. 19-20.

57   Passwater, Richard A. *Supernutrition.* New York: Pocket Books, 1977, pg. 63.

61   Kirschmann, Gayla and John. *Nutrition Almanac,* 4th edition. New York: McGraw-Hill, 1996, pps. 204-205.

63   Davis, Adelle. *Let's Eat Right to Keep Fit.* New York: Penguin Books, 1988.

Chapter Six

70 Gorman, Jack M., M.D. *The Essential Guide To Psychiatric Drugs.* New York: St. Martin's Press, 1995, pg. 193.

70 Basco, Monica Ramirez, Ph.D., and Rush, A. John, M.D. *Cognitive-Behavioral Therapy for Bipolar Disorder.* New York: The Guilford Press, 1996, pg. 88.

70 Schou, Mogens, M.D. *Lithium Treatment of Manic-Depressive Illness.* Basel: Karger, 1993, pps. 27-28.

73 Lemonick, Michael D. "The Mood Molecule," in *Time Magazine,* September 29, 1997, pps. 75-82.

73 Goodwin, Frederick K., M.D., and Jamison, Kay Redfield, Ph.D. *Manic-Depressive Illness.* New York: Oxford University Press, 1990, pg. 453.

73 Slater, S., deLa Vega, C. E., Skyler, J., and Murphy D. L. "Plasma prolactin stimulation by fenfluramine and amphetamine. *Psychopharmacol Bull* 12: 26-27, 1976.

81 Stahl, Stephen M. *Essential Psychopharmacology.* New York: Cambridge University Press, 1996.

82 *Nut. Rev.* 15, 185, 1957.

82 *Nut. Rev.* 4, 259, 1946.

82 Conney, A. H., et al. *Nature,* v. 184, Suppl. 6, 1959, pg. 363.

86 Murphy D. L., and Beigel, A. "Depression, elation and lithium carbonate responses in manic patient sub-groups. *Archives of General Psychiatry* 31: 643-654, 1974.

87 Fieve R. R., and Peselow, E. D. "Lithium: clinical applications." In: Burrows G. D., Norman, T. R., and Davies, B. (eds.) *Antidepressants. Drugs in Psychiatry* 1. Elsevier, Amsterdam, pps. 277-321, 1983.

87 Worrall, E. P., Moody, J. P., and Peet, M. "Controlled studies of the acute antidepressant effects of lithium." *British Journal of Psychiatry* 135: 255-262, 1979.

88 Baastrup, P. C., and Schou, M. "Lithium as a prophylactic agent against recurrent depression and manic-depressive psychosis." *Archives of General Psychiatry* 16: 162-172, 1967.

88 Angst, J., Weis, P., Grof, P., Baastrup, P. C., and Schou, M. "Lithium prophylaxis in recurrent affective disorders. *British Journal of Psychiatry* 116: 604-614, 1970.

88 Hullin, R. P., McDonald, R., and Allsopp, M. N. "Prophylactic lithium in recurrent affective disorders. *Lancet* 1: 1044-1046, 1972.

88 Baastrup, P. C., Poulsen, K. S., and Schou, M., et al. "Prophylactic lith-

ium: double-blind discontinuation in manic-depressive and recurrent-depressive disorders. *Lancet* 2: 230-236, 1970.

88   Coppen, A., Noguera, R., and Bailey, J., et al. "Prophylactic lithium in affective disorders: controlled trial. *Lancet* 2: 275-279, 1971.

89   Prien, R. F., Klett, C. J., and Caffey, E. M. "Lithium carbonate and imipramine in prevention of affective episodes. A comparison in recurrent affective illness." *Archives of General Psychiatry* 29: 420-425, 1973.

Chapter Seven

96   Ford, D. E., and Kamerow, D. B. "Epidemiological studies of sleep disturbances and psychiatric disorders: an opportunity for prevention?" *Journal of the American Medical Association* 262(11): 1479-1484, 1989.

97   Giles, D. E., Biggs, M. M., Rush, A. J., and Roffwarg, H. P. "Risk factors in families of unipolar depression, I: Psychiatric illness and reduced REM latency." *Journal of Affective Disorders* 14: 51-59, 1988.

98   Balch, James, M.D., and Balch, Phyllis A., C.N.C. *Prescription for Nutritional Healing*. Garden City Park, New York: Avery Publishing Group Inc., 1990, pg. 237.

100 Yanker, Gary, and Burton, Kathy. *Walking Medicine*. New York: McGraw-Hill, Inc., 1993, pps. 292-294.

102 Airola, Dr. Paavo. *How To Get Well*. Phoenix: Health Plus Publishers. 1974, pg. 237.

103 Bloomfield, Harold H., M.D. *TM: Discovering Inner Energy and Overcoming Stress*. New York: Dell Publishing Co., Inc., 1975, pg. 29.

106 Goldberg, Burton. *Alternative Medicine: The Definitive Guide*. Fife, Washington: Future Medicine Publishing, Inc., 1993, pg. 340.

Chapter Eight

114 Fink, Max, M.D. "Electroconvulsive Therapy" in *Handbook of Affective Disorders*, 1992.

114 Meduna, L. "General Discussion of Cardiazol Therapy." *American Journal of Psychiatry* 94, Suppl. 40, 1938.

114 Cerletti, U., and Bini, L. "Un nuovo metodo di shokterapia;" *Bulletin Accademia Medica di Roma* 64, 136-8, 1938.

114 Cronholm, B., and Ottoson, J. O. "Experimental Studies of the Therapeutic action of Electroconvulsive Therapy in endogenous depression." *Acta Psychiatrica Scandinavica*, Suppl. 145, 69-101, 1960.

114 Miller, D. H., Clancy, J., and Cumming, E. "A comparison between unidirectional current non-convulsive electrical stimulation given with Reiter's machine, standard alternating current electric shock (Cerletti method) and pentothal in chronic schizophrenia." *American Journal of Psychiatry* 109, 617-20, 1953.

114 Brill, N. Q., et al. "Relative effectiveness of various components of electroconvulsive therapy." *Archives of Neurology and Psychiatry* 81, 627-35, 1959.

114 Laurell, B. "Comparison of electric and flurothyl convulsive therapy with regard to anti-depressive effect." *Acta Psychiatric Scandinavica* Suppl. 145, 22-35, 1970.

115 Gelder, M. *Oxford Textbook of Psychiatry.* Oxford: Oxford University Press. 1983.

115 Barker, J. C., and Barker, A. A. "Deaths associated with electroplexy." *Journal of Mental Science* 105, 339-48, 1959.

115 Heshe, J., and Roeder, E. "Electroconvulsive therapy in Denmark." *British Journal of Psychiatry* 128, 241-5, 1976.

116 Freeman, C. P. L., and Kendell, R. E. "ECT: patients' experiences and attitudes." *British Journal of Psychiatry* 137, 8-16, 1980.

Chapter Nine

118 Kraepelin, E. *Manic Depressive insanity and paranoia* (translated by R. M. Barclay from the 8th Edition of *Lehrbuch der Psychiatrie,* Vols. III and IV). E. and S. Livingstone, Edinburgh. 1921.

119 Goldstein, Eda G. *Ego Psychology and Social Work Practice.* New York: The Free Press, 1995.

123 Paykel, E. S. *Handbook of Affective Disorders.* New York: The Guilford Press, 1992, pps. 213-215.

124 Beck, A. T. *Cognitive therapy and the emotional disorders.* International Universities Press, New York, 1976.

125 Basco, Monica Ramirez, Ph.D., and Rush, A. John, M.D. *Cognitive-Behavioral Therapy for Bipolar Disorder.* New York: The Guilford Press, 1996, pg. 94.

128 Chopra, Deepak, M.D. *Unconditional Life.* New York: Bantam Books, 1991, pg. 45.

129 Crichton, Michael. *Travels.* New York: Ballantine Books, 1988, pg. 55.

131 Ornish, Dean, M.D. *Love and Survival.* New York: HarperPerennial, 1998, pps. 24-25.

133   Goldstein, Michael J., and Miklowitz, David J. *Bipolar Disorder: A Family-Focused Approach.* New York: The Guilford Press, 1997.

Chapter Ten

138   James, William. *Principles of Psychology,* Vols. I and II. New York: Dover, 1950. Originally published 1890, Henry Holt.
139   Willard, Dallas. *The Divine Conspiracy.* New York: HarperCollins, 1998, pps. 80-81.
141   Whybrow, Peter C., M.D. *A Mood Apart.* New York: Basic Books, 1997, pg. 234.

Appendix C

149   Selye, Hans, M.D. *Stress Without Distress.* New York: New American Library, 1974, pg. 23.
150   Whybrow, P. C., and Hurwitz, T. "Psychological Disturbances Associated with Endocrine Disease and Hormone Therapy." In *Hormones, Behaviour, and Psychotherapy* (ed. E. J. Sachar). New York: Raven Press, 1976.
151   Cohen, F. "Cushing's Syndrome: A Psychiatric Study of 29 Patients." *British Journal of Psychiatry* 136: pps. 120-4, 1980.
151   Starkman, M. N., and Schteingart, D. E. "Neuropsychiatric Manifestation of Patients with Cushing's Syndrome." *Archives of Internal Medicine* 141, pps. 215-19, 1981.
151   Kind, D. "Die Psychiatrie der Hypophyseninsuffizienz Speziell der Simmondsschen Krankheit." *Forschritte der Neuologie-Psychiatrie* 26, pps. 501-63, 1958.
151   Petersen, P. "Psychiatric Disorders in Primary Hyperparathyroidism." *Journal of Clinical Endocrinology and Metabolism.* 28, pps. 1491-5, 1968.
151   Karpati, G., and Frame, B. "Neuropsychiatric Disorders in Primary Hyperparathyroidism: Clinical Analysis with Review of the Literature." *Archives of Neurology* 10, pps. 387-97, 1964.
152   Krauthammer, C., and Klerman, G. L. "Secondary Mania." *Archives of General Psychiatry* 35, pps. 1333-9, 1978.

Further Reading

I have classified into five groups books similar in content to my own.

Group A

These books are anthologies of papers written by professional scholars and researchers for other professionals in the field.

> Gelder, Gath, and Mayou, *Oxford Textbook of Psychology*, Oxford University Press, 1983.
> Goodwin and Jamison, *Manic-Depressive Illness*, Oxford University Press, 1990.
> Paykel, *Handbook of Affective Disorders*, The Guilford Press, 1992.

Group B

These books are written for fellow professionals and the lay public by professional psychiatrists who specialize in mood disorder. Their primary emphasis is to inform their audience of the biochemical revolution in psychiatry: to explain that Freudian psychology and talk therapy have taken a back seat to drug therapy in the treatment of mental illness. These books herald lithium as the wonder drug for manic depression. The last book, Whybrow's, discusses the latest antidepressants — in addition to lithium.

Fieve, *Moodswing*, Bantam Books, 1989.
Kline, *From Sad to Glad*, Ballantine Books, 1974.
Schou, *Lithium Treatment of Manic-Depressive Illness*, S. Karger, 1993.
Whybrow, *A Mood Apart*, Basic Books, 1997

Group C

These books are similar to mine in that they are written by individuals who have suffered from mood disorder. They are largely memoirs of moods and madness. They attempt to share what these mood swings are like and what one endures with this illness.

Berger, *We Heard the Angels of Madness*, William Morrow & Company, 1992.
Duke and Hochman, *A Brilliant Madness*, Bantam Books, 1993.
Duke, *Call Me Anna*, Bantam Books, 1988.
Colbert, *Depression & Mania: Friends or Foes*, Kevco Publishing, 1995.
Jamison, *An Unquiet Mind*, Alfred A. Knopf, 1995.
Kelly, *Manic Depression: Illness or Awakening*, Knowledge Unlimited Publishing, 1995.
Torrey, *Schizophrenia and Manic-Depressive Disorder*, Basic Books, 1994.
Wider, *Overcoming Depression and Manic Depression*, Wider Publishers, 1993.
Wren, *Thank God I'm Manic*, Rosemary Wren Productions, 1993.

Group D

These books are written for professional colleagues and the lay public; they offer practical information for bipolar patients and their families.

Basco and Rush, *Cognitive-Behaviorial Therapy for Bipolar Disorder*, The Guilford Press, 1996.
Copeland, *Depression Workbook: A Guide for Living with Depression and Mania*, New Harbinger Publications, 1992.

Goldstein and Miklowitz, *Bipolar Disorder: A Family-Focused Treatment Approach,* The Guilford Press, 1997.

Group E

As their titles suggest, the books in this last group focus on a particular aspect of the manic-depressive personality.

Hershman, *A Brotherhood of Tyrants: Manic Depression and Absolute Power,* Prometheus Books, 1994.

Hershman, *The Key to Genius: Manic Depression and the Creative Life,* Prometheus Books, 1988.

Jamison, *Touched with Fire: Manic-Depressive Illness and the Artistic Temperament,* The Free Press, 1993.

Index

About the Author

John T. Young earned his Bachelors Degree (1965) and Masters Degree (1968) in English from The University of Michigan. From 1969 to 1974 he held a Doctoral Fellowship in English at Miami University, Oxford, Ohio. Over the course of a distinguished teaching career that spanned thirty years, Young earned numerous awards for excellence. He was twice named to *Who's Who Among America's Teachers*.

Now retired from full-time teaching, Young works part-time for his local newspaper and serves as Adjunct Professor of English at Grand Valley State University. Recently, he was appointed to the Board of the Mental Health Foundation of Western Michigan. He also continues to enjoy the major passions of his life: his family, reading, writing, and golf.

Notes

Notes

Notes

Notes

ORDER FORM

Please send: _____ copies of

Sad Love Stories: A Study in Manic-Depressive Illness to:

Name: _____

Address: _____

City: _____ State: _____ Zip: _____

Telephone: (_____) _____

PRICE

$15.95 for the first book	_____ $15.95
$14.95 for each additional book	_____
Michigan Sales Tax: 6%	_____
Shipping: $4.00 for the first book	_____
$2.00 for each additional book	_____
TOTAL	_____

PAYMENT   Please pay by check payable to **Corshum Press**

                Send check and completed order form to:

                Corshum Press

                P.O. Box 883

                Ada, Michigan 49301

READER'S COMMENTS

To improve future editions of this book, please send what you consider
the strengths and weaknesses of this edition to:

Corshum Press

P.O. Box 883

Ada, Michigan 49301